THE ORIGIN OF RUSSIAN COMMUNISM

NICOLAS BERDYAEV

THE ORIGIN OF
RUSSIAN COMMUNISM

ANN ARBOR PAPERBACKS FOR THE STUDY OF COMMUNISM AND MARXISM

THE UNIVERSITY OF MICHIGAN PRESS

Sixth printing 1972
First edition as an Ann Arbor Paperback 1960
First published by Geoffrey Bles 1937
New edition, 1948
ISBN 0-472-06034-1 (paperbound)
ISBN 0-472-09034-8 (clothbound)
Published in the United States of America by
The University of Michigan Press and simultaneously in
Don Mills, Canada, by Longman Canada Limited
Translated from the Russian by R. M. French
Manufactured in the United States of America

CONTENTS

INTRODUCTION
THE RUSSIAN IDEA OF RELIGION AND
THE RUSSIAN STATE

I

Russian Communism is difficult to understand on account of its twofold nature. On the one hand it is international and a world phenomenon; on the other hand it is national and Russian. It is particularly important for Western minds to understand the national roots of Russian Communism and the fact that it was Russian history which determined its limits and shaped its character. A knowledge of Marxism will not help in this. The Russian people in their spiritual make-up are an Eastern people. Russia is the Christian East, which was for two centuries subject to the powerful influences of the West, and whose cultured classes assimilated every Western idea. The fate of the Russian people in history has been an unhappy one and full of suffering. It has developed at a catastrophic tempo through interruption and change in its type of civilization.

In spite of the opinion of the Slavophils it is impossible to find an organic unity in Russian history. The Russians held sway over too vast an expanse of territory—the danger from the East, from the Tartar invasions (from which it protected the West as well), was too great. And the danger from the West itself was also great.

We distinguish five different Russias in history: the Russia dominated by Kiev, the Russia of the Tartar period, the Russia of the Moscow period, the imperial Russia of Peter and finally the new Soviet Russia. It would not be true to say that Russia is a land of new culture, that not long ago she was still half barbarous; in a definite sense Russia is a land of ancient culture. The Russia of the Kiev period gave birth to a higher culture than that of the contemporary West. Already in the fourteenth century there existed

[7]

in Russia a classically perfect ikonography and a remarkable architecture. Russia of the Moscow period developed a very high culture in the plastic arts with an organic integrated style and highly finished forms of life. This was an Eastern culture—the culture of the Christianized Tartar Empire.

The culture of Moscow was developed in constant opposition to the Latin West and to foreign customs. But in the Muscovite Empire intellectual culture was very weak and lacked expression. The Muscovite Empire was almost without thought and speech, but during this period, in addition to the development of the plastic arts, the elemental basis of the life of the time was given significant form; and this was lacking in the Russia of Peter, though the latter awoke to the expression of ideas in words. Thinking Russia, which produced a great literature and sought after social justice, was dismembered and styleless and had no organic unity.

The inconsistency of the Russian spirit is due to the complexity of Russian history, to the conflict of the Eastern and Western elements in her. The soul of the Russian people was moulded by the Orthodox Church—it was shaped in a purely religious mould. And that religious mould was preserved even to our own day, to the time of the Russian nihilists and communists. But in the Russian soul there remained a strong natural element, linked with the immensity of Russia itself, with the boundless Russian plain. (1)[1]

Among Russians 'Nature' is an elemental power, stronger than among Western peoples, especially those of the most elaborated, i.e. Latin, culture. The nature-pagan element entered even into Russian Christianity. In the typical Russian two elements are always in opposition—the primitive natural paganism of boundless Russia, and an Orthodox asceticism received from Byzantium, a reaching out towards the other world.

A natural dionysism and a Christian asceticism are equally characteristic of the Russian people. A difficult problem presents itself ceaselessly to the Russian—the problem of organizing his vast

[1]For Author's Notes see p. 189 ff.

territory. The immensity of Russia, the absence of boundaries, was expressed in the structure of the Russian soul. The landscape of the Russian soul corresponds with the landscape of Russia, the same boundlessness, formlessness, reaching out into infinity, breadth.

In the West is conciseness; everything is bounded, formulated, arranged in categories, everything (both the structure of the land and the structure of the spirit) is favourable to the organization and development of civilization. It might be said that the Russian people fell a victim to the immensity of its territory. Form does not come to it easily, the gift of form is not great among the Russians. Russian historians explain the despotic character of Russian government by this necessary organization of the boundless Russian plain. Kluchevsky, the most distinguished of Russian historians, said, 'The state expands, the people grow sickly.' In a certain sense this remains true also of the Soviet-Communist government, under which the interests of the people are sacrificed to the power and organization of the Soviet state.

The religious formation of the Russian spirit developed several stable attributes: dogmatism, asceticism, the ability to endure suffering and to make sacrifices for the sake of its faith whatever that may be, a reaching out to the transcendental, in relation now to eternity, to the other world, now to the future, to this world. The religious energy of the Russian spirit possesses the faculty of switching over and directing itself to purposes which are not merely religious, for example, to social objects. In virtue of their religious–dogmatic quality of spirit, Russians—whether orthodox, heretics or schismatics—are always apocalyptic or nihilist. Russians were true to type, both in the seventeenth century as Dissenters and Old-ritualists, and in the nineteenth century as revolutionaries, nihilists and communists. The structure of spirit remained the same. The Russian revolutionary intelligentsia inherited it from the Dissenters of the seventeenth century. And there always remains as the chief thing the profession of some orthodox faith; this is always the criterion by which membership of the Russian people is judged.

[9]

After the fall of the Byzantine Empire, the Second Rome, the greatest Orthodox state in the world, there awoke in the Russian people the consciousness that the Russian Muscovite state was left as the only Orthodox state in the world and that the Russian people was the only nation who professed the Orthodox Faith. It was the Monk Filofei who expounded the doctrine of Moscow as the Third Rome. He wrote to the Tsar Ivan III: 'Of the third new Rome' . . . 'Of all kingdoms in the world, it is in thy royal domain that the holy Apostolic Church shines more brightly than the sun. And let thy Majesty take note, O religious and gracious Tsar, that all kingdoms of the Orthodox Christian Faith are merged into thy kingdom. Thou alone, in all that is under heaven, art a Christian Tsar. And take note, O religious and gracious Tsar, that all Christian kingdoms are merged into thine alone, that two Romes have fallen, but the third stands, and there will be no fourth. Thy Christian kingdom shall not fall to the lot of another.'

The doctrine of Moscow the Third Rome became the basic idea on which the Muscovite state was formed. The kingdom was consolidated and shaped under the symbol of a messianic idea. The search for true, ideal kingship was characteristic of the Russian people throughout its whole history. Profession of the true, the Orthodox Faith, was the test of belonging to the Russian kingdom. In exactly the same way profession of the true communist faith was to be the test of belonging to Soviet Russia, to the Russian communist state. Under the symbolic messianic idea of Moscow as the Third Rome there took place an acute nationalizing of the Church. Religion and nationality in the Muscovite kingdom grew up together, as they did also in the consciousness of the ancient Hebrew people. And in the same way as messianic consciousness was an attribute of Judaism it was an attribute of Russian Orthodoxy also. But the religious idea of the kingdom took shape in the formation of a powerful state in which the Church was to play a subservient part. The Moscow Orthodox kingdom was a totalitarian state. Joseph Volotsky was the founder of state Orthodoxy. Ivan the Terrible, who was a remarkable theoretician of absolute monarchy, taught that a Tsar must not only govern the state, but also save souls. It is interesting to note that the Muscovite period was the period of Russian history in which the smallest number of saints was produced.

The best period in the history of the Russian Church was the period of the Tartar yoke, when spiritually it was most independent and displayed a strong social sense. (2) Œcumenical consciousness was weakened in the Russian Church to such an extent that Russians ceased to regard the Greek Church, from which the Russian people received their Orthodoxy, as a true Orthodox Church; they began to regard it as a crippled expression of the true faith. Greek influences were taken by popular religious thought as corruptions penetrating into the only Orthodox kingdom in the world. The Orthodox faith was the Russian faith; what was not Russian faith was not Orthodox faith. When, under the Patriarch Nikon, the correction of mistakes in the service books according to Greek models and some insignificant changes in ceremonial were undertaken, they called forth a violent protest from popular religion. In the seventeenth century there took place one of the most important events in Russian religious history, the Old-ritualist schism.

It is a mistake to think that this religious schism was the outcome simply of the Russian people's beliefs about ceremonial and that the struggle was waged merely over the question of making the sign of the cross with two or with three fingers, and over other details in the ordering of divine worship. There was something deeper than that in the schism. The question was this: is the Russian kingdom a true Orthodox kingdom, i.e. is the Russian people fulfilling its messianic vocation? Of course, unenlightenment, illiteracy and superstition and the low cultural level of the clergy played a large part in it. But an event so vast in its effects as the schism cannot be explained by those things alone. A suspicion awoke in the people that the Orthodox kingdom, the Third Rome, was being impaired, that a betrayal of the true faith was taking place. Antichrist had seized on the hierarchy of Church and State alike. Popular Orthodoxy broke with both. True Orthodoxy retired underground. From this arose the legend of the City of

Kitezh which was hidden beneath a lake. The people were seeking the City of Kitezh. A keen apocalyptic consciousness came into being in the left wing of the schism, the section known as 'the Priestless'. Schism became a characteristic phenomenon of Russian life. In the same way the Russian revolutionary intelligentsia of the nineteenth century was to become sectarian and to think that the forces of evil had seized power.

Both among the Russian masses and among the Russian intelligentsia will be found the search for a kingdom founded on justice. In the visible kingdom injustice reigns. In the Muscovite kingdom, aware of itself as the Third Rome, was mingled the Kingdom of Christ, a kingdom of justice, with ideas of a mighty state ruling by injustice. The schism was the exposure of the inconsistency, the result of the mingling. But the popular mind was unenlightened, often superstitious; in it Christianity was mingled with paganism. The schism gave the first blow to the idea of Moscow as the Third Rome. It showed that all was not well with the Russian messianic consciousness. The second blow was given by the reform of Peter.

II

Peter's reform was a fact so decisive for all subsequent Russian history that our currents of thought in the nineteenth century were distinguished by the value they assigned to it. One must now regard as equally untrue and out of date both the Slavophil and the Western points of view about Peter's work. The Slavophil saw in it the betrayal of the original national basis of Russian life, a violation and interruption of its organic development. The Westernizers saw nothing original and distinctive whatever in Russian history; they considered Russia as only a backwater in enlightenment and civilization. The Western European type of civilization was for them the only type, and must be universal. Peter showed Russia the ways of Western enlightenment and civilization.

The Slavophils were wrong, because Peter's reform was absolutely inevitable. Russia could no longer exist as a closed country, in a backward condition both military and naval, and economic, without education and technical civilization. In such circumstances the Russian people not only could not fulfil its great mission, but its very independence was exposed to danger. The Slavophils were wrong for this reason too, that it was precisely in the Petrine period of its history that Russian culture bloomed, Pushkin and the great period of Russian literature appeared, thought awoke and the Slavophils themselves became possible. Russia was obliged to break out of its isolation and join in the swirling life of the world. Only in such ways could the Russians make their contribution to the life of the world.

The Westernizers were wrong, because they denied any original distinctive character to the Russian people and Russian history, they clung to naïvely simple views of the progress of enlightenment and civilization, and saw no mission of any sort for Russia, except the necessity of catching up with the West. They did not see, what for that matter even the Slavophils saw, the violation of the soul of the people, which Peter perpetrated. Peter's reform was unavoidable, but he achieved it in a way which did terrible violence to the soul of the people and to their beliefs. And the people answered this violence by founding a legend of Peter as Antichrist.

Peter was a revolutionary from above; and not without reason is he considered a bolshevik in type. Peter's methods were absolutely bolshevik. He wanted to destroy the old Muscovite Russia, to tear up by the roots those feelings which lay in the very foundation of its life. With that object in view he did not stop at the execution of his son, who held to the old-fashioned ways. The methods adopted by Peter in dealing with the Church and the old religion are very reminiscent of the methods of the bolsheviks. He did not like the old Muscovite piety and was especially severe on the adherents of the old rites and on the Old Believers. Peter ridiculed the religious feelings of the old days; he organized a mock Council with a mock Patriarch. This very much recalls the anti-religious activities of the godless in Soviet Russia. Peter founded a synodal régime to a large extent copied from the German Protestant form, and he brought about the final subjection of the Church to the State.

It ought to be said, however, that it was not Peter who was to blame for the degrading of the Russian Church during the Petrine period of Russian history. Already in the Muscovite period the Church was in slavish dependence on the State. The moral authority of the hierarchy among the people had fallen before Peter's time. The religious schism dealt a terrible blow to that authority. The level of education and culture among the ecclesiastical hierarchy was very low. On that ground, too, Peter's reform of the Church was a necessity. But it was carried out by violence and with no mercy on the religious feelings of the people.

A comparison might be made between Peter and Lenin, between the Petrine and the bolshevik revolutions. They display the same barbarity, violence, forcible application of certain principles from above downwards, the same rupture of organic development, and repudiation of tradition, the same *étatism*, hypertrophy of government, the same formation of a privileged bureaucratic class, the same centralization, the same desire sharply and radically to change the type of civilization. But the bolshevik revolution, by terrible violence, liberated forces that were latent in the masses and summoned them to take their share in making history; therein lies its significance. While Peter's revolution, having strengthened the Russian State and urged Russia along the way of Western and World enlightenment, widened the gulf between the people and the upper classes, the cultured and ruling class. Peter secularized the Orthodox kingdom and guided Russia into the way of enlightenment. This process took place in the upper levels of Russian society, among the nobility and civil servants, while at the same time the people went on living by the old religious beliefs and feelings. The autocratic power of the Tsar, in fact, assuming the form of a Western enlightened absolutism, kept in the people's eyes its old religious sanction as a theocratic authority.

The weakening of the spiritual influence of the official Church was an inevitable result of Peter's reform and the triumph of Western enlightenment. Rationalism appeared even in the Church hierarchy itself. The well-known Metropolitan of Peter's time, Theophan Prokopovitch, was in reality a Protestant of the rationalistic type. But in the Petrine period this had its compensation in a series of saints such as the Muscovite epoch had not known, in *starchestvo*,[1] in hidden spiritual life.

The Western education among the upper ranks of Russian society in the eighteenth century was alien to the Russian masses. The Russian ruling class of the eighteenth century was superficially influenced by the teachings of Voltaire on the one part and by mystical Freemasonry on the other. But the people went on living by the old religious beliefs and regarded the gentry as an alien race. That enlightened disciple of Voltaire, Katharine II, who corresponded both with him and with Diderot, finally established those forms of serfdom which called forth the protests of the pained conscience of the nineteenth century Russian intelligentsia.

The influence of the West struck primarily at the masses and strengthened the privileged classes. People like Radishchev were exceptions. Only in the nineteenth century did the influence of the West on the Russian educated intelligentsia give birth to love of the people and to liberationist movements. But even then the educated and cultured classes seemed alien to the people. Nowhere, apparently, was there such a gulf between the upper and lower classes as in Petrine, imperial Russia, and not another single country lived at the same time in such different centuries, from the fourteenth to the nineteenth and even to the coming twenty-first century.

Russia of the eighteenth and nineteenth centuries lived a completely inorganic life. In the soul of the Russian people a struggle between East and West was waged, and that struggle is continuing in the Russian revolution. Russian communism is a communism of the East. The influence of the West during the two centuries of its action failed to subdue the Russian people. We shall see that the Russian intelligentsia was absolutely non-Western in type, however much it swore by Western theories.

The Empire founded by Peter grew outwardly; it became the largest in the world. It had an outward enforced unity, but there was no inward unity; inwardly it was broken into fragments. Government and people were rent apart, people and intelligentsia,

[1]See footnote on p. 134.

[15]

and the nationalities which were gathered together in the Russian Empire were sundered from each other. The Empire with its Western type of imperial absolutism less than anything realized the idea of the Third Rome. The very title 'Emperor' substituted for 'Tsar' was, in Slavophil opinion, a betrayal of the Russian idea. The despotic Nicholas I was of the Prussian officer type. At court and in the upper ranks of the bureaucracy German influences were very strong.

The fundamental opposition was between the idea of an Empire, a mighty State of the military-police type, and the religious, messianic idea of a Tsardom which descended to become the possession of the masses, and then, under a transformed aspect, reached the intelligentsia. The conflict between the idea of Empire as expressed by the Government and the outlook of the intelligentsia was to be fundamental for the nineteenth century. The Government was to make itself more and more alien from the intelligentsia among the cultured classes of society, in which a revolutionary temper was to begin to grow. The nobility, which was the leading and specially cultured class at the beginning and even in the middle of the nineteenth century, in the second half of the century was to sink in cultural level, become reactionary, and be forced to give way to an intelligentsia drawn from many classes who would bring with them another and new type of culture. The absence of unity and of an integral culture is shown in this—that the intelligentsia and spiritual currents of the nineteenth century are divided into decades and each decade brings with it new ideas and tendencies, a new spiritual tenor of life. And for all that, the Russian nineteenth century produced one of the greatest literatures in the world, and an intense, original, very free thought.

The bulk of the Russian people—the peasantry—lived in the grip of serfdom. Inwardly they lived by the Orthodox Faith and that gave them power to bear the sufferings of life. The people always considered serfdom as a wrong and an injustice, but they assigned the blame for this injustice not to the Tsar, but to the ruling class, the nobility. The religious conception of the Tsar's authority was so strong among the people that they lived in the hope that the Tsar would protect them and put an end to the injustice when he learned the whole truth.

In accordance with their own ideas of property, the Russian peasantry always thought it wrong that the nobles should possess vast tracts of land. Western ideas of property were alien to the Russian people; they were but feebly understood even by the nobility. The soil was God's, and all who toiled and laboured at it might enjoy the use of it. A naïve agrarian socialism was always an accepted principle among the Russian peasants.

To the cultured classes—to the intelligentsia—the mass of the people remained a sort of mystery of which the secret was yet to be discovered. They believed that in the still silent inarticulate people lay concealed a great truth about life, and that the day would come when the people would say their say. The intelligentsia, divorced from the masses, lived under the fascination of a people, mystic, because wedded to the soil, of that which the *narodnik*[1] writers for seventy years called 'the authority of the soil'. By the nineteenth century Russia had assumed the form of an immense, unbounded peasant country, enslaved, illiterate, but with its own popular culture based on a faith, with a ruling noble class, idle and with little culture, which had lost its religious faith and its sense of nationality; with a Tsar at the top, in relation to whom a religious belief was retained; with a strong bureaucracy and a very thin and fragile layer of culture.

Social classes in Russia have always been weak, subjected to the State; they were even formed by State authority. The only vigorous elements were the monarchy, which had taken the form of Western absolutism, and the masses. The cultured layer felt itself crushed by these two forces. The intelligentsia of the nineteenth century stood over an abyss which at any moment might open and swallow it. The best, the most cultivated part of the Russian nobility was aware of the abnormality, the wrongness of its position, the blame attaching to it in the face of the masses.

By the nineteenth century, the Empire was very sick, both

[1]This word, and the abstract noun 'narodnichestvo' derived from it, are explained by the author at the beginning of Chap. III, p. 58.

spiritually and economically. The bringing together of principles which are antinomies and polar opposites is characteristically Russian. Russia and the Russian people can be characterized only by contradictions. On the same grounds the Russian people may be characterized as imperial-despotic and anarchic freedom-loving, as a people inclined to nationalism and national conceit, and a people of a universal spirit, more than others capable of œcumenic views; cruel and unusually humane; inclined to inflict suffering and illimitably sympathetic. This contradiction is established by all Russian history and by the eternal conflict of the instinct of imperial might with the instinct of the people's love of freedom and justice.

In spite of the opinion of the Slavophil, the Russian people were endowed with political sense. This remains true even for the Soviet State, and at the same time it is a people from whom issued constantly the Cossack freebooters, the risings of Stenka Razin and Pugachev, a revolutionary intelligentsia, anarchic, a people who sought for a kingdom of righteousness not of this world. That righteousness was not to be found in the vast Empire State founded through terrible sacrifices. This was felt by the masses and by the best part of the nobility and by the newly-educated intelligentsia.

Russia of the nineteenth century was self-contradictory and unhealthy; in it there was oppression and injustice, but psychologically and morally it was not a bourgeois country and it set itself against the bourgeois countries of the West. In this unique country political despotism was united with great freedom and breadth of life, with freedom in manner of life, with absence of barriers, imposed conventions and legalism.

CHAPTER I

THE FORMATION OF THE RUSSIAN INTELLI-
GENTSIA AND ITS CHARACTER. SLAVOPHIL-
ISM AND WESTERNIZATION

I

To understand the sources of Russian communism and make clear to oneself the character of the Russian revolution, one must understand that singular phenomenon which in Russia is called 'intelligentsia'. Western people would make a mistake if they identified the Russian intelligentsia with those who in the West are known as 'intellectuals'.

'Intellectuals' are people of intellectual work and creativeness, mainly learned people, writers, artists, professors, teachers and so on. The Russian intelligentsia is an entirely different group; and to it may belong people occupied in no intellectual work, and generally speaking not particularly intellectual. Many Russian scholars and writers certainly could not be reckoned as belonging to the intelligentsia in the strict sense of the word. The intelligentsia reminds one more of a monastic order or sect, with its own very intolerant ethics, its own obligatory outlook on life, with its own manners and customs and even its own particular physical appearance, by which it is always possible to recognize a member of the intelligentsia and to distinguish him from other social groups.

Our intelligentsia were a group formed out of various social classes and held together by ideas, not by sharing a common profession or economic status. They were derived to begin with mainly from the more cultured section of the nobility, later from the sons of the clergy, small government officials, the lower middle class, and, after the liberation, from the peasants. That then is the intelligentsia; its members were of different social classes, and held together solely by ideas, and, moreover, by ideas about sociology. In the second half of the nineteenth century the stratum of society which is simply called cultured is developed into a new type and is given the name 'intelligentsia'. This type has its characteristic traits which belong to all its present representatives.

There were typical Russian features in the intelligentsia and it is a wholly mistaken opinion which regarded it as denationalized and severed from the Russian soil. Dostoyevsky, although he did not like revolutionary ideas, admirably understood the true Russian character of the revolutionary member of the intelligentsia and called him 'the great wanderer of the Russian land'. Lack of roots in the soil, a break with all class life and traditions, are characteristic of the intelligentsia, but even these qualities in them took a characteristically Russian form.

The intelligentsia was always carried away by some idea or other, for the most part by social ideas, and devoted itself to them supremely. It acquired the power of living by ideas alone. Owing to Russian political conditions, the intelligentsia found itself divorced from practical social work, and that easily led to social day dreaming. In the Russia of autocracy and serfdom, the most radical socialist and anarchist ideas were developed. The impossibility of political action led to this, that politics were transferred to thought and literature. It was the literary critics who were the leaders of social and political thought and character. The intelligentsia assumed that sectarian character which is so natural to all Russians. It lived in schism from its actual environment, which it considered evil, and within it a fanatical sectarian ethic was elaborated.

The thoroughly true-to-type intolerance of the Russian intelligentsia was self-protective; only so could it preserve itself in a hostile world, only thanks to its fanaticism could it weather persecution and retain its characteristic features. Extreme dogmatism, a thing to which Russians are fundamentally disposed, was characteristic of the Russian intelligentsia, dominated as it was by social motives and a revolutionary frame of mind which fostered the type of man whose sole speciality was revolution. Russians possess a particular faculty for assimilating Western ideas and doctrines and giving them an original form. But the assimilation of Western ideas and doctrines by the Russian intelligentsia was for the most part made a matter of dogma. What was scientific theory in the West, a hypothesis, or in any case a relative truth, partial, making no claim to be universal, became among the Russian intelligentsia a dogma, a sort of religious revelation.

Russians are always inclined to take things in a totalitarian sense; the sceptical criticism of Western peoples is alien to them. This is a weakness which leads to confusion of thought and the substitution of one thing for another, but it is also a merit and indicates the religious integration of the Russian soul. Among the Russian radical intelligentsia there existed an idolatrous attitude to science itself. When a member of the Russian intelligentsia became a Darwinist, to him Darwinism was not a biological theory subject to dispute, but a dogma, and anyone who did not accept that dogma (e.g. a disciple of Lamarck) awoke in him an attitude of moral suspicion. The greatest Russian philosopher of the nineteenth century, Solovëv, said that the Russian intelligentsia professed a faith based upon the strange syllogism: man is descended from a monkey, therefore we ought to love one another. In this totalitarian and dogmatic way the Russian intelligentsia accepted and lived through Saint Simonism, Fourierism, Hegelianism, materialism, Marxism—and Marxism in particular.

Generally speaking, Russians but poorly understood the meaning of the relative, the fact that historical progress advances by stages, the differentiation of various spheres of culture. Russian maximalism is due to this. The Russian spirit craves for wholeness. It cannot reconcile itself to the classification of everything according to categories. It yearns for the Absolute and desires to subordinate everything to the Absolute, and this is a religious trait in it. But it easily leads to confusion, takes the relative for the Absolute, the partial for the universal, and then it falls into idolatry. It is a property of the Russian spirit especially to switch over the current of religious energy to non-religious objects, to the relative and partial sphere of science or social life. This explains a great deal.

As early as the eighteenth century the type of Russian intelligentsia began to emerge. Radishchev, the author of *A Journey from Petersburg to Moscow*, was the first. His words 'My soul was wounded by the suffering of humanity' establish the type of Russian intelligentsia. Radishchev was brought up on French eighteenth century philosophy, on Voltaire, Diderot, Rousseau. But he had no anti-religious tendency, as had many Voltairians of that time. French ideas entered into the Russian spirit and became sympathy and philanthropy. Radishchev could not tolerate serfdom and the degradation and suffering of the masses. At the time that Radishchev's book appeared, Katharine II was already in the grip of a reactionary mood. Radishchev was arrested and condemned to death on account of his book, but the sentence was commuted to imprisonment. In the same way, Novikov, a notable worker for Russian enlightenment in the eighteenth century, a man of the mystical type, a Christian of very moderate political views was arrested and imprisoned in the Peter and Paul fortress. In this fashion the formation of the Russian intelligentsia was greeted by Russian authority. The first steps of the Russian intelligentsia along the paths of enlightenment—not revolution—brought with them sacrifice and suffering, imprisonment and hard labour.

Radishchev held views which for his time were rather daring and radical and he was one of the forerunners of the revolutionary intelligentsia and of Russian socialism. But in the eighteenth century Russian thought was not yet original. The nineteenth century was to be the century of original thought and self-consciousness. It was also to be the century of inward revolution. To us self-consciousness meant revolt against the actual facts around us, against imperial Russia. Enlightenment destroyed the old belief in the Orthodox kingdom and the search for the kingdom took another direction; the Russian mission was conceived in another way. The loneliness of Russian cultured and freedom-loving people in the first half of the nineteenth century was extraordinary. (3) There were cultured people, but no cultured environment. The people of that time complain that they are surrounded by unenlightenment, that no one understands them and no one sympathizes with them. The bulk of the Russian nobility and official class were very uncultivated, illiterate and devoid of any of the higher interests of life. It was that 'mob' of which Pushkin speaks. The picture of Chatsky in *The Misfortune of Being Too Wise* depicts that loneliness of the best people, especially of the learned and cultured at that period.

At the beginning of the nineteenth century, in the time of Alexander I, Russia lived through a cultural renaissance. That was the Golden Age of Russian poetry, the time of mystical tendencies and of the Decembrist movement. Alexander I himself was a 'Tsar-intelligent', a seeker after truth all his life, in his youth an enemy of autocracy and serfdom, but a man of divided mind and no great strength. The renaissance of those days affected but a meagre part of the nobility. Cultured people and seekers after truth had to live as small groups and societies. Masonry tinged with mysticism was very widespread in the time of Alexander and was an important educative influence. Masonry was the first form that the self-organization of society assumed. Into that mould flowed the particularly tense spiritual life of that time.

The beginning of the nineteenth century was a period in which the surface of the Russian spirit was broken into, so that it became susceptible to ideas of all sorts, to spiritual and social movements. It was a time of universalism, of inter-confessional Christian associations. Then also Russian *fsyechelovechnost*[1] began to take shape and became characteristic of the nineteenth century. Through the Napoleonic war Russia was brought into immediate touch with the West; Russian officers visited Europe and came back with a broadened mental outlook. Alexander I was himself a Russian *fsyechelovek*. He met Owen and talked to him about a new structure of society; he worshipped with Quakers. But this did not prevent the end of his reign from being marked by a grim reaction. The Russian soul was getting itself ready for the nineteenth century. But there was no wholeness and unity in Russian life. There was a gulf between the upper cultural level of the

[1]See the note at the end of the chapter.

nobility, who then served in the Guards, and the average bulk of that class. In that upper level there were spiritual and literary movements; from it arose the Decembrist movement which aimed at liberation from autocracy and serfdom. But it all went on in such a small and secluded section that it could not really change Russian life. The Decembrist rising, which witnesses to the disinterestedness of the élite of the nobility, was doomed to failure and was sternly crushed. The chief actors in the movement were executed or exiled to Siberia by Nicholas I.

A large number of the Decembrists held moderate and even monarchist views. But Pestel, who represented the extreme left wing and was the author of *Russian Justice*, may be called the first Russian socialist before the socialists, as Hertzen put it. In him there was already seen that will to power and violence which in the twentieth century appeared in the communists. But Pestel's socialism was, of course, agrarian. He was a republican, a partisan of the sovereignty of the people, and at the same time a centralist. He was not a liberal, and was inclined to despotism. But at the very time of the Decembrist movement the vast mass of the Russian nobility was unenlightened, idle, and led an unreflecting life. Belonging to the middle Russian nobility he began by serving in the Guards. He soon retired and settled in the country, where he had no occupation and made himself conspicuous by all sorts of oddities and petty despotism.

This was the greatest failure of the Petrine period. That age produced the type of 'superfluous people'—either Rudins or Oblomovs. And the best of the 'superfluous people' were those who sadly recognized their superfluity, like several of Turgeniev's heroes. In Pushkin alone, a unique Russian of the renaissance, there gleams the possibility of another attitude to life. Pushkin combined in himself, as it were, the consciousness of the intelligentsia and the consciousness of empire. He wrote revolutionary verse, and at the same time he was the poet of Russian imperialism. After the suppression of the Decembrist rising, after the accession of Nicholas I, everything tended towards the growth of schism and revolution. The Russian intelligentsia was definitely shaped into a schismatic type. It will always speak of itself as 'we'; and of the State, of authority, as 'they'.

The Russian cultured class was suspended over an abyss, crushed by two fundamental forces, autocratic monarchy above and an unenlightened mass of peasantry beneath. Russian thought, without basis and rebellious, in the nineteenth century was inwardly free and audacious; it was not chained to a grim past and to tradition, but outwardly it was cramped and even persecuted.

The impossibility in the political circumstances of direct social work led to this, that all activity passed into literature and thought, where every question was posed and decided very radically. Limitless social day dreaming, with no connection with actual reality, was the result. Russians were disciples of Saint Simon, Fourier, Proudhon, at a time when serfdom and autocracy still existed in Russia. They were most extreme and totalitarian disciples of Hegel and Schelling when there was no philosophical culture whatever in Russia, and philosophical thought lay under suspicion. Cultured Russians loved endless discussions lasting through whole nights, and arguments about world questions, among small groups, in the salons of the 'thirties and 'forties.

The first awakening of independent thought and self-consciousness—in the nineteenth century—came with Chaadaev, a man of exceptional gifts, but who wrote almost nothing. He was idle, as were most Russian gentlemen. His unusually keen and powerful thought was set forth in a single *Philosophical Letter*. This was a whole philosophy of history. The theme was fundamental to Russian nineteenth century thought. The first question over which independent Russian thought pondered was one in which lies the problem of Russia and the peculiarity of its line of progress: Is she East or West?

This first Russian historical philosopher, Chaadaev, was an officer of the Hussar life-guards, in retirement, just as the first and most distinguished Russian theologian, Khomyakov, was an officer of the horse-guards. Chaadaev's philosophy of history was a revolt against Russian history, against the Russian past and the Russian present. Peter's work awoke Russian thought and Russian creativeness. Hertzen said that the Russian people's answer to Peter's reforms was the appearance of Pushkin. To this we must add that they also replied with the appearance of Westernizing and Slavophil thought. All Russian nineteenth century thought which was occupied with general questions of world outlook was either Westernizing or Slavophil, that is, it answered the question: Ought Russia to be West or East? Must she follow Peter's path, or turn back to the time before him, to Muscovite Russia? Chaadaev came out decidedly as a Westernizer, and his Westernism was a cry of patriotic anguish. He was the typical nineteenth century Russian of the cultured upper class. His rejection of Russia—of Russian history—was a typically Russian rejection; his Westernism was religious, in distinction from subsequent forms of Westernism; he was very sympathetic with Roman Catholicism and saw in it the active, unifying, organizing strength of history, and in it he saw salvation for Russia.

Russian history presented itself to him as devoid of meaning, and with no connecting links, belonging neither to the East nor to the West. It was the reflection of that loss of cultural style which was so characteristic of Peter's age. Chaadaev considered Russia a lesson and a warning to other peoples. The Government saw in Chaadaev a revolutionary. But in actual fact he was near in his ideas to de Maistre, Bonalde and Schelling, with the last of whom he corresponded and who held him in high esteem. The highly cultured Chaadaev could not reconcile himself to the fact that he was condemned to live in an uncultured society, in a despotic state, which gripped an unenlightened people as in a vice and did nothing to enlighten them. Chaadaev expressed thought which one must regard as fundamental to Russian self-consciousness. He spoke of the latent powers of the Russian people, powers which had not yet revealed themselves. This might appear to condemn the Russian people in so far as it applied to the past. They had created nothing great in history, had fulfilled no great mission. But it might also, when applied to the future, become a great hope and faith in the future of the Russian people as being called to realize a great mission.

Precisely on that latent power and backwardness of the Russian people the whole nineteenth century will base the hope that the Russians are called to solve problems which are difficult for the West to solve as a result of the burden of its own past; for example, the social question. That was what it meant for Chaadaev. The Russian Government replied to the first awakening of Russian thought by announcing that Chaadaev was a madman. He was subjected to medical examination. In this way Chaadaev was crushed and silenced. But later on he wrote *A Madman's Apology*, and in it he expressed thoughts about Russian messianism which were typically Russian. Judgment upon the past was one thing, hope for the future was another. Precisely in the strength of the latent power lying in its immense untapped forces, the Russian people was called to say its own original word to the world, to fulfil its great mission. In Chaadaev may already be found much fundamental Russian thought.

In their cleavage from contemporary life, in their protest against the injustice of Russian life, cultured Russians attempted an appeal to Roman Catholicism and to find salvation in that. A characteristic figure in this connection is Pecherin, who went abroad and became a Roman Catholic monk. He combined Roman Catholicism with Utopian socialism. At that period attempts were being made to give socialism a Christian basis; they were influenced by Lammenais; the intelligentsia still had a religious framework. In one of his poems Pecherin wrote: 'How sweet to hate one's own native land and eagerly to await its annihilation'—typical Russian words—words of despair behind which is hidden a love of Russia. In the West, Pecherin, already a Roman Catholic monk, was yearning for Russia and believed that Russia was to inaugurate a new cycle of world history.

II

The basic Western influence, by which Russian nineteenth century thought and culture were moulded to a remarkable degree, was the influence of German romanticism and idealism at the beginning of the century, especially the influence of Schelling and Hegel who became almost Russian thinkers. This influence did not mean a slavish imitation such as the influence of Voltaire had meant in the eighteenth century. German thought was taken actively and worked over into a Russian type of thought. It is particularly necessary to say this of the Slavophils, among whom the influence of Schelling and Hegel fertilized theological thought, just as the influence of Plato and the Neoplatonists formerly fertilized the theological thought of the Eastern doctors of the Church. Khomyakov founded an original Orthodox theology into which worked-over themes of German idealism enter.

Like the German romantics, Russian thought strove after *wholeness* and did so more consistently and radically than the romantics, who themselves lost wholeness. The wholeness of the Christian East is set in opposition to the rationalist fragmentariness of the West. This was first pointed out by I. Kireevsky and it became a fundamental Russian theme rooted in the depths of Russian character. Russian communist atheists assert wholeness, totalitarianism, no less than the Orthodox Slavophils. Psychologically, Russian orthodoxy is wholeness, totalitarianism; the Russian Westernizers to whom the religious type of Slavophil was alien, were influenced by Hegelianism, which to them was simply a totalitarian system of thought and life embracing absolutely everything. When Belinsky and Bakunin were Hegelians they were precisely that sort of Hegelian. A young Russian, belonging to the idealist generation of the 'thirties and 'forties, professed a totalitarian Schellingism or totalitarian Hegelianism in relation to the whole of life, not only the life of thought and social life, but also personal life, in relation to love or natural feeling. Belinsky, a revolutionary by nature and temperament, who gave a basis to the Russian revolutionary and socialist outlook, at one time became a conservative under the influence of Hegel's philosophy. He felt himself bound to accept the reasonableness of reality; he grasped Hegel's thought that everything real is rational.

Creative originality in religious and philosophical thought was shown by the Slavophils. They established the mission of Russia as distinct from that of Western peoples. The originality of the Slavophils lay in this: they endeavoured to comprehend the distinctiveness of the Eastern Orthodox type of Christianity which lay at the basis of Russian history. Although the Slavophils sought for organic foundations of history and paths of development, yet they also were sectarian and lived in schism from their actual environment. They rejected the Imperial Russia of Peter; they did not feel at home among the actual circumstances of the time of Nicholas I; and authority regarded them with suspicion and hostility, notwithstanding their Orthodoxy and monarchist principles.

There was nothing in common between the official theory of the Russian national spirit, worked out in the time of Nicholas I as the accepted point of view of the Government, and the Slavophil understanding of nationality. The official system was based on three principles: Orthodoxy, autocracy and nationality, and the Slavophil system recognized the same three principles. But the spirit was not the same. It was absolutely clear that for the official system the principle of autocracy was primary; Orthodoxy and nationality were subservient to that. It was also clear that nationality in the official sense was of a dubious character and under the influence of the worst sides of Western political absolutism. Nicholas I was of the Prussian officer type. The Orthodoxy, too, was not spiritual and inward; it was political and became a means to an end.

These principles had an entirely different meaning for the Slavophils. They acknowledged first of all the absolute primacy of the religious principle, and they sought an Orthodoxy which was purified, not distorted and perverted by historical influences. They also strove for the realization of a genuinely national spirit. They saw a vision of the Russian people freed from the distortion which they attributed to Western rationalism and political absolutism. Their attitude to the State was entirely different from anything to be found in the system of official nationalism. The Slavophils were opposed to the State. There was even a strong element of anarchism in them. They considered the State an evil and government a sin. They defended monarchy on the ground that it is better for one man to be defiled by possessing authority, which is always sinful and vile, than the whole people. (4) The Tsar has no right to authority, and no more has anyone else. But he is constrained to bear the burden of authority which the people have laid upon him.

The Slavophils considered that the Russian people had no gift for politics. It has a religious and spiritual vocation and wishes to be free from political affairs in order to realize that vocation. Of course, this theory contradicts the fact that the Russian people have founded the biggest State in the world, and indicated a break with the traditions not only of Peter but also of the Grand Princes of Moscow. But the Slavophils were therein expressing one of the poles of Russian consciousness, a characteristic trait of the intelligentsia of the nineteenth century and of all Russian literature. The Slavophils were the founders of that nationalism which was so characteristic of Russian nineteenth century thought and afterwards took reactionary forms. The Slavophils believed in the people, in justice that belonged to the people, and for them the people was first and foremost the muzhik, who kept the Orthodox Faith and the national tenor of life. The Slavophils were warm defenders of the Commune, which they regarded as organic and as the original Russian structure of economic life among the peasantry, as all the *narodniks* thought. They were decided opponents of the ideas of Roman Law on property. They did not regard property as sacred and absolute; owners of property they regarded as stewards only. They repudiated Western, bourgeois, capitalist civilization. And if they thought that the West was decaying, it was because it had entered upon the path of that bourgeois civilization, because in it the unity of life had been split asunder. The Slavophils already anticipated the distinction between culture and civilization which has become popular in the West from the writings of Spengler.

In spite of the conservative element in their outlook, the Slavophils were warm defenders of freedom of the person, of conscience, of thought and of speech; and they were democrats in an original sort of way, recognizing the principle of the sovereignty of the people. Khomyakov, in his poetry, exposed the historical sins of Russia, not only of the Russia of Peter, but of the Russia of the time before him, and was even more trenchant than the Westernizers. The Slavophils and the Westernizers were both friends and foes. Hertzen said: 'We are like the two-faced Janus; we have one love of Russia, but it is not the same love. For some Russia is first and foremost a mother, for others—a child.' The Slavophils and Westernizers of the 'thirties and 'forties belonged to one circle; they argued in the same drawing-rooms which witnessed the contests of Hertzen and Khomyakov. It was only later that they definitely parted. The intolerant Belinsky was already refusing to meet his friend K. Aksakov.

The best, the most thoughtful and cultured people of the nineteenth century did not live in the present, which was abhorrent to them; they lived in the future, or in the past. Some, the Slavophils, dreamed of an ideal Russia before Peter's time; others, the Westernizers, dreamed of an ideal West. But even the Slavophils' conservative handling of the distant past was but a Utopia of a perfect régime, the perfect life, just as was the Westernizers' presentation of the West, which they knew none too well. The Westernizers were frequently agents of enlightenment and civilization; and that is the least interesting type. The more interesting type of Westernizer was that which made a Russian re-hash of Western ideas, in particular of French social teaching. In Russia, if Hegel and Schelling were taken up in a totalitarian, entire and maximalist fashion, so also were Saint Simon and Fourier. In the camp of the radical wing of the Westernizers, the influence of French socialism and French literature was strong, especially that of Georges Sand, who had an immense influence in shaping emotional life in Russian cultured circles, in fashioning the Russian attitude to freedom and sincerity of feeling, the Russian protest against violence, conventionality and insincerity of feeling. The plan for realizing social righteousness was worked out according to Saint Simon and Fourier. And, of course, the French themselves had no such passion for these ideas.

At the end of the 'forties a group used to meet at the house of a Russian landowner called Petrashevsky. It passed judgment on social problems and planned a new and better organization of humanity. Most of the members of the group followed Fourier and Saint Simon. Their ideas for the reorganization of humanity were very radical, but the character of their conversations was most peaceful and harmless. (5) They concerned themselves with no revolutionary activity of any sort. At that time no revolutionary activity existed in Russia, nor could it. Everything happened in the realm of thought. Most of all, of course, they desired the liberation of the peasants. The utopian socialism of the group was idyllic. They postulated three stages in the development of socialist ideas in Russia: the stage of utopian socialism, *narodnik* socialism and scientific or Marxian socialism.

Petrashevsky was a very typical Russian landowner, afire with the ideas of utopian socialism. He said: 'Unable to find anything either in women or in men worthy of my adherence, I have turned to devote myself to the service of humanity.' In that was expressed a most characteristic frame of mind of the Russian revolutionary intelligentsia—the love of the man far off, not the love of one's neighbour. It is to this man far off that Petrashevsky reached out, to the happiness of humanity. He believed in the happiness of humanity. Petrashevsky's naïve utopianism was expressed in the fact that on his estate he set up a *phalanstery*[1] for the peasants on the Fourier model. But the peasants burnt that *phalanstery*. The fact is symbolic. In the same way, in the 'seventies, the peasants refused to accept the socialist intelligentsia who went to them with offers of self-denying service. When questioned, Petrashevsky even maintained that the *phalanstery* was wholly possible in the Russia of serfdom and autocracy. The opinion was characteristic of the utopian age of socialism.

The most extreme revolutionary tendency in Petrashevsky's group was represented by N. Speshnev who apparently served Dostoyevsky as a model when he drew the picture of Stavrogin in *The Possessed*. Speshnev was an atheist and a communist and came

[1] A communal house.

very near to Marxism. Dostoyevsky took part in Petrashevsky's group, although he was sceptical of the possibility of realizing Fourier's utopian socialism. The peaceful gatherings of Petrashevsky's group ended sadly, as everything ended sadly in Russia at that time. All its members were arrested and twenty-one were condemned to death, commuted to penal servitude. Among them was Dostoyevsky, who had to live through the moment of condemnation to be shot. The Petrashevsky case could not but strengthen the revolutionary temper of the Russian intelligentsia. Russian socialism will no longer be merely idyllic. The figures of Nechaev and Tkachev are to appear. It is very interesting to note that the first Marxists in the world were Russians. Russian Marxism, as a movement, arose only in the second half of the 'eighties, but individual Russian Marxists existed already at the end of the 'forties in Paris. Thus the Steppe landowner, N. I. Sazonov, was the first Russian Marxist in Paris, and perhaps one of the first disciples of Marx in general. (6)

Marx, who generally speaking did not like Russia and the Russians, writes with amazement from Paris, that followers of his had made their appearance who were Russian Steppe landowners. He felt some mistrust of these too early Marxists. Marx was to go through much unpleasantness later on with Bakunin and carry on a controversy with him about the First International, although it would seem that from the beginning Bakunin influenced the Marxist conception of the mission of the proletariat. (7) In any case, the Russian capacity for a supreme enthusiasm for social ideas is very germane to our subject. Right through the nineteenth century the Russians had an irresistible inclination to socialism, and everything prepared a passion for communism among them. Hertzen's fate is a subject of immense interest in the history of Russian self-consciousness, of the Russian national idea, and of the Russian social idea.

III

Hertzen was a Westernizer, who argued with the Slavophils in the drawing-rooms of the 'forties. Although he also passed through Hegelianism, he soon went over to Feuerbach. The fundamental influence upon him was not German, but the influence of French socialist literature. Hertzen's socialist outlook was elaborated under the influence of the French socialists. The German socialism, then coming to the fore, i.e. Marxism, was alien to him. Hertzen belonged to those Russian Westernizers who dreamed passionately of the West and idealized it. Hertzen lived abroad; he was one of the first Russian emigrants. He came upon the West in the atmosphere of the Revolution of 1848, and at first he was attracted by it and founded great hopes on it. But it was his fate to live through the bitter disillusionments which followed the Revolution of 1848, in the West and among Western people generally. His passion for the West was typically Russian, as was his disillusionment in the West. Many Russians after him lived through similar disillusionments. Hertzen was amazed and hurt by the pettiness of the West; he noted this petty bourgeois spirit even among socialists. He was among the first to see the possibility of a bourgeois socialism. The ideal of the Knight was altered into the ideal of the small shopkeeper. The arraignment of the bourgeois spirit of the West is a typically Russian theme. The Slavophils gave expression to it, in other terms. K. Leontev, the reactionary, will rebel against the pettiness of the West just as Hertzen, the revolutionary, did.

Hertzen, as distinct from other representatives of the left wing, did not profess an optimistic theory of progress. On the contrary, he defended a pessimistic philosophy of history. He did not believe in the rationality and goodness of a historical process which moved towards the realization of higher good. This is the original and interesting thing about Hertzen. He recognized the higher value of human personality, although it is crushed by the progress of history. He laid the foundation of the original Russian individualistic socialism which was to be represented in the 'seventies by N. Mikhailovsky. Socialist individualism is opposed to bourgeois individualism. Hertzen could not see what forces there were in Western Europe to be opposed to the empire of pettiness. The Western European workman had this pettiness of mind and, therefore, he could not save the West from it. Hertzen, the emigrant, deprived till his death of any possibility of a bodily return to his native land, returned thither in spirit. However horrible the autocratic régime of Nicholas I, its serfdom, and its illiteracy, yet it was precisely in Russia, in the Russian people, that there lay hidden the latent power to fashion a new and a better life, not petty and not bourgeois. Hertzen sees these potentialities in the Russian muzhik, in the muzhik's grey sheepskin coat, in the peasant Commune. In the Russian peasant-world was hidden the possibility of bringing together the principle of personality and the principle of community and social life. Hertzen was a humanist sceptic; religious beliefs were alien to him. Belief in the Russian people, in truth latent in the muzhik, is for him the final anchor of salvation. Hertzen became one of the originators of Russian *narodnichestvo*, a peculiarly Russian phenomenon. In the person of Hertzen Russian Westernism approached Slavophilism in certain respects.

In the Westernizing camp there occurred a split into the *narodnik* socialists and the liberals. Hertzen and the *narodnik* socialists believed in a special path of progress for Russia, in its vocation to realize social justice better and earlier than the West. They believed it was possible for Russia to escape the horrors of capitalism. The Westernizing liberals thought that Russia must pass along the same road as Western Europe, The *narodniks* repudiated politics; they thought that politics would push Russia along the trite Western road of development; they recognized the primacy of the social over the political. This also is a characteristically Russian theme. Hertzen, Bakunin, even such shocking revolutionaries as Nechaev and Tkachev were, in a certain sense, nearer the Russian idea than the enlightened Westernizers and liberals. All the subsequent atheism of the Russian revolutionary socialist and anarchist tendencies was Russian religiousness turned inside out, Russian apocalyptic. It is most important to note that the liberal tradition has always been weak in Russia and that we have never had a liberalism with moral authority or which gave any inspiration. The authors of the liberal reforms of the 'sixties had, of course, some significance, but their liberalism was exclusively practical and businesslike; they produced no theory whatever, a thing which the Russian intelligentsia always needs.

NOTE.—*Fsyechelovechnost* means ability to share the point of view of all nations or types or individual persons (see Dostoyevsky's speech at the unveiling of the Pushkin Monument). *Fsyechelovek* (p. 23) is the person with this ability.

CHAPTER II
RUSSIAN SOCIALISM AND NIHILISM

I

Although Belinsky was a man of the 'forties and belonged to the generation of the Slavophils and Westernizers, yet he was perhaps the first who gave expression to the type of revolutionary intelligentsia, and at the end of his life he formulated the fundamental principles of its general outlook which were developed later on in the 'sixties and 'seventies. In the first place, Belinsky was not a Russian gentleman like all the Slavophils and Westernizers, like Hertzen and Bakunin. He belonged to a different social class, he was a *raznochinets*.[1] There were traits in his spiritual make-up which were typical of the intelligentsia; he was intolerant, fanatical, inclined to sectarianism, passionately devoted to ideas; he was constantly elaborating a view, not such as pure knowledge required, but as a basis for his aspirations towards a better and more righteous social order. Belinsky was a man of remarkable gifts and a notable susceptibility to ideas, but the level of his education was not high. He was almost entirely without knowledge of foreign languages and became acquainted with the ideas to which he was devoted at second hand. He came to know Hertzen principally through what Bakunin told him.

Belinsky passed through all the stages in enthusiasm for ideas usual in Russian cultured circles of that time. He was in turn a disciple of Fichte, Schelling and Hegel, and later went over to Feuerbach; he felt the influence of French literature and French socialist thought. He was above all an admirable literary critic; he was the first to value Pushkin, Gogol, and the early creative work of our great novelists. He himself possessed artistic susceptibility

[1] 'Person belonging neither to any guild, nor to the merchant class nor to the nobility.'

and was capable of aesthetic judgment, and he became the ancestor of that type of literary critic who was destined to play an immense part in the history of the thought of the intelligentsia. In Belinsky there was the characteristically Russian search for an integral outlook which will give an answer to all the questions of life, unite the theoretical and practical reason, and give a philosophical basis to the social ideal. Integrated truth, as later expressed by N. Mikhailovsky, who was also in the line of descent from Belinsky, is both truth in the abstract and that truth which finds expression in justice. The same idea of wholeness will be found in N. Federov in a religious setting, and in Marxist Leninism. The Russian critical publicists will always preach an integrated outlook, will always connect truth and righteousness, will always be teachers of life. Belinsky was the first specially gifted representative of this type. He already affirms the social side of the work of the literary critic. Russian social thought was concealed under the form of literary criticism, because under the conditions of censorship it could not otherwise find expression. In the evolution and revolution of ideas through which Belinsky lived, the crisis which Hegelianism reached in his mind is of particular interest and importance. (8) Russian thought passed through two such crises in regard to Hegelianism: one in Khomyakov which was religious, the other in Belinsky which was social. (9)

The fundamental problem which interested Russians in the 'forties who were attracted by Hegel was the problem of their relation to 'actuality'. Hegel's doctrine of the rationality of actual fact, which in Hegel himself was entirely a matter of logic and meant the recognition of the fact that only the rational was authentically real, was in Russia a matter of most tense and painful experience and was falsely interpreted. It is well known that Hegel can be understood in a conservative sense or in a revolutionary sense; he originated a right and a left current of thought. He was the philosopher of the Prussian State, in which he saw the embodiment of absolute spirit, and at the same time through his dialectic he brought a revolutionary dynamic into thought and gave birth to Marx. The Russian Hegelians of the 'forties at first understood Hegel in the conservative way, and interpreted his thought of the rationality of 'actuality' to mean that one must reconcile oneself to one's actual environment—the period of Nicholas—and recognize reason in it. Belinsky and Bakunin, men of revolutionary outlook on life, passed through such a period of conservative Hegelianism. Russian romantic idealists of the 'forties escaped from actual social conditions into the world of thought, imagination, literature, into the reflected world of ideas. They suffered from the ugliness and injustice of their environment, but were powerless to alter it. Discord with their actual environment made Russians inactive, and produced the type of 'superfluous people'. Hegelianism included a possibility of relation to actual fact which might have a double meaning. The identity of life and thought consists not only in the carrying over of life into thought but also in the carrying over of thought into life.

At the end of the 'forties, in Belinsky's last period, a stormy and passionate relation to actual social conditions did occur, but leading not to reconciliation but to conflict. Conflict presupposes a relation to actual fact, to reality. A dream relation to life makes conflict impossible. But in Belinsky this took the form of a crisis in his Hegelianism. All the left revolutionary Russian thought broke away from Hegelianism until the coming of Marxism, which turned towards Hegel anew, but now interpreted his dialectic in a revolutionary sense. In his latest period Belinsky went over to revolutionary socialism and militant atheism. This found expression in the remarkable letters to Botkin, which could not be printed in the old Russia. The revolt against Hegel is a revolt on behalf of living human personality, and the conflict for living human personality resolved itself into a conflict for a socialist structure of society. Thus was formulated the characteristically Russian type of individualistic socialism.

Above all, Belinsky, with his usual impetuosity, rebels against an abstract idealism remote from concrete life, which sacrifices the individual to the general, the living human person to the world soul. 'The fate of the subject, the individual, the person,' he writes, 'is more important than the fate of the whole world or the well-

[39]

being of the Chinese Emperor.' 'I reverence your philosopher's gown,' he observes to Hegel, 'but with all due respect to your philosophical philistinism, I have the honour to inform you that if it were given me to climb to the highest rung in the ladder of development, even there I would ask to be rendered an account for all the victims of the circumstances of life and history, for all the victims of chance, of superstition, of the Inquisition, of Philip II and so on and so on. Otherwise I would fling myself down headlong from that highest rung. I do not want happiness even as a gift unless I have peace of mind about my brothers by blood, bone of my bone, and flesh of my flesh. They say that disharmony is a condition of harmony. Maybe that is very pleasant and consoling for lovers of music, but it is certainly not so for those to whom fate allots the part of expressing disharmony in their experience.' These words are very important to the subsequent Russian problem. In them is posed the problem of evil, the problem of the justification of suffering, which is the fundamental Russian problem and the source of Russian atheism; it is the problem of the cost of progress, which will play a large part in the social thought of the 'seventies.

Belinsky anticipated Dostoyevsky; he had already lived through Ivan Karamazov's problem of the tears of a child; in him was conceived Dostoyevsky's argument in the *Legend of the Grand Inquisitor*. It seems sometimes as though in the thoughts of I. Karamazov Dostoyevsky had in mind Belinsky, whom he knew very well personally and with whom he disputed a good deal. Belinsky lived through despair and bitterness after his disillusion in idealism. He became a revolutionary, an atheist and a socialist. It is an important fact that in Belinsky Russian revolutionary socialism was combined emotionally with atheism. The source of this atheism was sympathy with mankind, the impossibility of reconciling oneself with the idea of God in view of the excessive evil and suffering of life. Such atheism arises from moral feeling, from love of what is good and righteous. Dostoyevsky will reveal this peculiar religious psychology. From sympathy with mankind, from revolt against the general (idea, reason, spirit, God) which has oppressed the living individual man, Belinsky became a socialist. He is an excellent witness to the moral-psychological sources of Russian socialism. Rebellion against the general for the sake of the individual, in him, passes over into a fight for the general in a new sense, for humanity, for its social organization. Belinsky fails to notice that having repudiated all that 'general' which had previously oppressed mankind, he was rapidly subjecting the individual to a new 'general'. And it seemed to him that this new 'general' to which he paid reverence, since a Russian cannot but pay reverence to something or other, he affirmed for the sake of individual personality. The same thing is to happen in the 'nineties. 'A social spirit!—or death!' cried Belinsky. 'What is it to me that the "general" lives, when the individual suffers! Repudiation is my God!'

In Russia at the end of the 'forties, there already existed that same process of thought which was formed in Germany in the left wing of Hegelianism, in Feuerbach and in Marx. There is a break with abstract idealism and a transference to actual concrete fact. Belinsky is permeated, in his own words, with a Marat's love of humanity. 'I become terrible', he writes, 'when I get some mystical absurdity or other into my head.' The Russian in general is like that; he often gets some 'mystical absurdity' into his head. These words of Belinsky's are very remarkable. From his sympathy with mankind, Belinsky was ready to preach tyranny and brutality. Bloodshed was unavoidable. In order to bring happiness to the greater part of mankind you may cut off the heads of hundreds of thousands. Belinsky was the forerunner of bolshevik morals. He says that people are so stupid that you must drag them to happiness by force. He admits that if he were Tsar he would be a tyrant on behalf of justice. He is disposed to dictatorship. He says the time will come when there will be no rich and no poor. Belinsky started the assertion that the Russians are an atheist people. But he still preserves a love for the Christ of the poor and unhappy. Belinsky writes Gogol a letter full of indigantion *à propos* of his book *Correspondence with Friends*. This letter, of course, could not be printed and was passed round from hand to hand. He branded Gogol as a traitor and a preacher of slavery. From a religious point of view he was wrong, but from a social point of view he was right.

Belinsky is the central figure in the history of Russian thought and self-consciousness in the nineteenth century. And he, more than any other, must be regarded as an intellectual ancestor of Russian communism and as one of its predecessors; certainly more than Hertzen and others of the 'forties and even of the 'sixties. He comes near to communism not only in his ethical thought but also in his social views. He is not a typical *narodnik*; he recognizes a positive importance in industrial development, he is even ready to admit the importance of the bourgeoisie, whom he cannot bear, exactly like the Russian Marxists later on.

In Belinsky may be studied the inward motives giving birth to the general outlook on life of the Russian revolutionary intelligentsia, which remained dominant for a long while and finally produced Russian communism, though in a different historical setting. These motives must be seen above all in a passionate indignant protest against the evil, violence and suffering of life, in sympathy with the unhappy, the destitute and the downtrodden. But as a result of pity, sympathy and the impossibility of bearing suffering, Russians became atheists. They became atheists because they could not accept a Creator Who made an evil, incomplete world full of suffering. They themselves desired to make a better world in which there should be no such wickedness and suffering. In Russian atheism there were thoughts akin to Marcion. But Marcion thought that the Creator of the world was an evil God, while the Russians, in a different intellectual age, thought that there was no God at all, or if He did exist that He would be an evil God. This is in Belinsky. Bakunin gives the impression of a fighter against God from motives akin to Marcionism. In Lenin this reaches its culmination. In the earliest origins of Russian atheism there lay a lofty human feeling which reaches exaltation. But in the final result, in militant godlessness when it came into power, Russian communism replaced the human feeling by its opposite. This was foreseen by Dostoyevsky.

Two lines of thought may be recognized in Belinsky. In the first place he turns his attention to the living human individual, to the suffering he is undergoing, and desires above all to assert that he is worthy of and has a right to life in its fulness. He rebels against the 'general', against the world spirit against idealism, on behalf of this living human person. But the direction of his attention very quickly changes, and the person is swallowed up in the social whole. It is society, the new society which can be established only by way of revolution, that can rescue the human individual person from the intolerable suffering and subjection. The larger part of society, constituting 'the people', endures this unjust suffering and subjection. But the focussing of the attention upon society and the necessity of changing it leads him to forget that very same human individual person, the fulness of his life, and his right to the spiritual content of life. The problem of society finally replaces the problem of man. Revolution overthrows the 'general' which had oppressed the human individual person, but makes him subject to a new 'general', to a society which demands for itself the complete submission of man. Such is the fateful development of religious-socialist and atheistic thought. Russian atheism, which was linked with socialism, is a religious phenomenon. In its foundations there lay a love of justice. Belinsky was already permeated with the sectarian spirit which is so characteristic of the Russian revolutionary intelligentsia.

One cannot call Belinsky a *narodnik* in the strict sense of the word. He did not share the characteristic *narodnik* belief in 'the people'. But in him were already formulated two principles which lay at the base of *narodnik* socialism—the principle of the supremacy of human personality and the principle of the communal socialist organization of human society. Personality and people—these were two fundamental ideas of Russian *narodnik* socialism. Hertzen was much more characteristic of *narodnik* socialism. He was better known in the West than Belinsky; he lived abroad; he edited *The Bell* in London; he was connected with the Western socialist movement and his books were translated into foreign languages. He was much more individualistic and humanist than Belinsky. But, as was said above, he was disillusioned in the West, and looked for salvation in the Russian muzhik, whom Belinsky certainly did not idealize. In Belinsky the potential Marxist already existed. The amazing thing is that in the Russian peasantry, living as they were in conditions of serfdom and devoid of the most elementary enlightenment, Hertzen saw a greater expression of the principle of personality than in the European who had become a bourgeois. In the Russian people the principle of personality was combined with the principle of community. Living in a foreign country Hertzen became the founder of *narodnik* socialism, which reached its highest development in the 'seventies. Hertzen believed that socialism could be brought into being more easily and better in Russia than in the West, and that it would not be bourgeois. Like many *narodniks* he was opposed to a political revolution which might drive Russia into the bourgeois path of development.

To be a socialist in those days meant to demand economic reforms, to despise liberalism, and to regard the development of capitalist industry as the chief evil, because it destroyed the conception of the peasant order of life as the highest type of society. Frequently this meant a sympathy with dictatorship, even with monarchy. The *narodnik* socialists were ready to support the monarchy in Russia if it would stand for the defence of the people against the nobility and the growing bourgeoisie. During his life abroad Hertzen, in the pages of *The Bell*, congratulated Alexander II on his action in liberating the peasants. But Hertzen, in spite of all his revolutionary socialist ideas, in spite of his situation as an emigrant, seemed alien to the generation of the 'sixties. He was a man of the 'forties, a cultured Russian barin, a humanist and a sceptic, but not a nihilist. He was not typical of the revolutionary intelligentsia, much less typical than Belinsky. Chernishevsky, who developed ideas of *narodnik* socialism akin to Hertzen, speaks of him with contempt, as a barin of the 'forties, who always goes on thinking that he is arguing with Khomyakov in the drawing-rooms of Moscow. In the 'sixties new social groups, and especially seminarists, came to the fore among the intelligentsia; the nobility ceased to dominate, and a sterner, more ascetic, spiritual type made its appearance, more realist and active. Those idealists who really belonged to the 'forties, but appeared in the 'sixties as the 'superfluous people', now seemed men of a bygone age. The nihilists came on the scene.

II

Nihilism is a characteristically Russian phenomenon; in its Russian form it is unknown in Western Europe. In the narrower sense of the word, nihilism is the intellectual liberation movement of the 'sixties, and Pisarev is recognized as its chief exponent. The Russian nihilist was sketched by Turgeniev in Bazarov. But in actual fact nihilism is a much wider thing than that for which Pisarev stands. It is to be found in the subsoil of Russian social movements, although nihilism in itself is not a social movement. There is a nihilist basis in Lenin, although he lives in another epoch. 'We are all nihilists,' says Dostoyevsky. Russian nihilism denied God, the soul, the spirit, ideas, standards and the highest values. And none the less nihilism must be recognized as a religious phenomenon. It grew up on the spiritual soil of Orthodoxy; it could appear only in a soul which was cast in an Orthodox mould. It is Orthodox asceticism turned inside out, and asceticism without Grace. At the base of Russian nihilism, when grasped in its purity and depth, lies the Orthodox rejection of the world, its sense of the truth that 'the whole world lieth in wickedness',[1] the acknowledgement of the sinfulness of all riches and luxury, of all creative profusion in art and in thought. Like Orthodox asceticism, nihilism was an individualist movement, but it was also directed against the fulness and richness of life. Nihilism considers as sinful luxury not only art, metaphysics and spiritual values, but religion also. All its strength must be devoted to the emancipation of earthly man, the emancipation of the labouring people from their excessive suffering, to establishing conditions of happy life, to the destruction of superstition and prejudice, conventional standards and lofty ideas, which enslave man and hinder his happiness. That is the one thing needful, all else is of the Devil. In the intellectual

[1] I St. John, 5.19.

sphere, one must find an ascetic satisfaction in the natural sciences, which destroy the old beliefs, and overthrow prejudices, and in political economy which inculcates the organization of a more righteous social order.

Nihilism is the negative of Russian apocalyptic. It is a revolt against the injustices of history, against false civilization; it is a demand that history shall come to an end, and a new life, outside or above history, begin. Nihilism is a demand for nakedness, for the stripping from oneself of all the trappings of culture, for the annihilation of all historical traditions, for the setting free of the natural man, upon whom there will no longer be fetters of any sort. The intellectual asceticism of nihilism found expression in materialism; any more subtle philosophy was proclaimed a sin.

The Russian nihilists of the 'sixties—and I have in mind not only Pisarev but also Chernishevsky, Dobrolyubov and others—were Russian prophets of enlightenment. They declared war against all historical traditions; they opposed 'reason', the existence of which as materialists they could not recognize, to all the beliefs and prejudices of the past. But the Russian prophets of enlightenment, in accord with the maximalist character of the Russian people, always became nihilists. Voltaire and Diderot were not nihilists. In Russia, materialism assumed an entirely different character from its Western form. Materialism was turned into a peculiar sort of dogmatic theology. This is a striking fact about the materialism of the communists. But already in the 'sixties materialism had assumed this theological tinge; it became a dogma of moral obligation and behind it was concealed a distinctive nihilist asceticism. A materialist catechism was framed, and was adopted by the fanatical circles of the left Russian intelligentsia. Not to be a materialist was to be taken as a moral suspect. If you were not a materialist, then you were in favour of the enslavement of man both intellectually and politically. The attitude of the Russian nihilists to science was idolatrous. Science, by which was to be understood principally the natural sciences, which at that time were presented in materialist colours, became an object of faith; it was turned into an idol. There were admirable scholars in Russia at that date who in themselves constituted a special phenomenon. But the nihilist prophets of enlightenment were not men of science. They were men of belief—and dogmatic belief. The methodical doubt of Descartes suits the nihilists, and indeed the Russian nature in general, but little. The typical Russian cannot go on doubting for very long; his inclination is to make a dogma for himself fairly quickly, and to surrender himself to that dogma whole-heartedly and entirely. A Russian sceptic is a Western type in Russia. There was nothing sceptical in Russian materialism; it was a faith.

In nihilism still another trait of the Russian Orthodox type was reflected in a distorted view, the lack of a solution of the problem of culture due to the Orthodox background of Russian mentality. Ascetic Orthodoxy was doubtful about the justifiability of culture; it was inclined to see sinfulness in cultural creativeness. This found expression in the painful doubt felt by the great Russian writers about the justifiability of their own literary work. Religious, moral and social doubt of the justification of culture is a most characteristically Russian theme. Doubt has been constantly expressed among us as to whether philosophical and artistic creativeness is justifiable. The problem of the cost at which culture is purchased will be dominant in the social thought of the 'seventies. Russian nihilism was a withdrawal from a world which 'lieth in wickedness', a break with the family and with all settled and established life. Russians accepted this break more easily than Western peoples. They considered the State, law and traditional morals sinful, for these things had been used to justify the enslavement of man.

More remarkable than anything is the fact that Russians, when nihilism had shaped them, readily sacrificed themselves and went to penal servitude and the gallows. They were striving after a future, but for themselves they had no hope whatever, either in this earthly life or in the life everlasting which they denied. They did not understand the Mystery of the Cross, but they were in the highest degree capable of sacrifice and renunciation. In this respect they compared favourably with the Christians of their day, who displayed very little capacity for sacrifice, and so repelled men from Christianity. Chernishevsky, who was a genuine ascetic in life, said that he preached liberty, but for himself he would never avail himself of any sort of liberty whatever, lest it should be thought that he defended liberty with a selfish purpose. (10) The wonderful capacity for sacrifice in men of a materialist view of life is evidence of the fact that nihilism was a distinctively religious phenomenon.

It was not by chance that seminarists, children of priests and those who passed through the Orthodox school played a great part in Russian nihilism. Dobrolyubov and Chernishevsky were sons of arch-priests and had studied in a seminary. The ranks of the 'left' intelligentsia among us were filled to a large extent by members of the clerical class. The significance of this fact is twofold. In the theological school the seminarist acquired a certain configuration of spirit in which ascetic denial of the world played a large part. At the same time, among the seminarists of the second half of the 'fifties and the beginning of the 'sixties, a violent protest against the decadent Orthodoxy of the nineteenth century was coming to a head, against the unseemliness of the lives of the clergy, and against the obscurantist atmosphere of the clerical schools. Seminarists were beginning to be permeated by the emancipating ideas of education, but permeated after the Russian fashion, that is to say, in an extremist, nihilist manner. No small part in this was played by the *ressentiment* of the seminarists to the culture of the nobility. At the same time a thirst for social justice was awakening in the young, and for them it meant the birth of Christianity in a new form. The seminarists and *raznochinsti*[1] brought with them a new build of character, sterner, ethical, exacting and exclusive, formed by a severer and more painful school of life than that in which the cultured members of the nobility had grown up. This new young generation changed the type of Russian culture. The type of culture in the men of the 'sixties, Dobrolyubov, Chernishevsky, the nihilists, the growing revolutionary intelligentsia, was somewhat low in comparison with that of the cultured nobility of the 'thirties and 'forties, the culture of Chaadaev, Iv. Kireevsky,

[1]See footnote on p. 37.

[48]

Khomyakov, Granovsky and Hertzen. Culture always develops and reaches more finished forms in aristocratic circles. When it becomes democratic and is diffused among other classes of society, its standard is lowered, and only later, as the human material is worked over, can culture rise higher again. That same process went on in Russia on a small scale among the intelligentsia of the 'sixties, and on a wide, national scale it took place at the Russian revolution. The change in the type of culture was expressed primarily in the different objects towards which it was directed. This had already been anticipated by Belinsky in the latest period of his development. The 'idealists' of the 'forties were interested mainly in the humane sciences, philosophy, art, literature. The nihilists of the 'sixties were chiefly interested in the natural sciences and political economy, and thus these became the interests also of the communist generation of the Russian revolution.

In the understanding of the genesis of Russian nihilism in the wide sense of the word and the Russian revolutionary spirit of the 'sixties, the figure of Dobrolyubov is of great interest. In him is seen the sort of soul in which revolutionary and nihilist ideas were born. It was the kind of soul from which saints are made. That may be said of Dobrolyubov and of Chernishevsky alike. Dobrolyubov left behind him a Diary in which he describes his childhood and youth. He had a purely Orthodox religious upbringing. In his childhood and even in early youth he was very religious. The cast of his soul was ascetic. He had a strong sense of sin and was disposed to frequent confession. The most insignificant sins caused him pain. He could not forgive himself if he ate too much jam, slept too long and so on. He was very devout. He loved his parents tenderly, especially his mother, and he could not become reconciled to her death. Dobrolyubov was a pure, stern, serious man, without any of that lightness of touch which gave such a charm to the cultured nobility. And then this devout, ascetic soul, serious to the degree of harshness, lost his faith, appalled by the evil, the injustice, and the suffering of life. He could not reconcile himself to the fact that with so evil a world, full of injustice and suffering, there exists an all-good and all-powerful Creator. Here is the destructive Marcion theme at work. Dobrolyubov is stunned by the fact that his beloved mother dies.

Nor can he reconcile himself to the low level of life among the Russian clergy, its lack of spirituality, its obscurantism, its absence of any application of Christianity to life. He feels himself surrounded by 'the kingdom of darkness'. His principal essay, written *à propos* of Ostrovsky, is entitled *A Ray of Light in the Kingdom of Darkness*. Man must himself bring light into the kingdom of darkness. What is needed is enlightenment, a revolutionary change in the whole order of life. Dobrolyubov was a critic; he wrote about literature. He did not go to such extremes as Pisarev in the repudiation of æsthetics, but even for him æsthetics were a luxury, and on ascetic grounds he rejected the superfluous luxury of æsthetics. He desired earthly happiness for man, and after he lost his faith he knew no other purpose in life. But he himself knew no happiness, his life was joyless, and he died of consumption almost in his youth. One can imagine Russian nihilism only as a youth movement; nihilism in the elderly has a repulsive character.

N. Chernishevsky dominated the thought not only of the radical intelligentsia of the 'sixties, but also of succeeding generations. The halo which surrounded his name in penal servitude contributed very greatly to his popularity. Chernishevsky was charged with drawing up proclamations to the peasantry, the charge against him being supported by forgery and false evidence. He was condemned to seven years' penal servitude, and after that spent twelve years in Eastern Siberia under extremely severe conditions. He bore Siberia and penal servitude as a genuine ascetic. Chernishevsky was a very gentle person; he had a Christian soul and there were marks of saintliness in his character.(11) This harrying of Chernishevsky was one of the most shameful actions of the Russian government of the old régime. Chernishevsky, like Dobrolyubov, was the son of an arch-priest. His earliest education was theological, and he was brought up in a seminary. He was a very learned person, a veritable encyclopædist; he knew both theology and philosophy down to the philosophy of Hegel; he knew history and the natural sciences; but he was chiefly an economist. As an economist Marx ranked him very high. He had gifts which might have made him a specialist, and if they did not actually do so, it was simply because he was attracted by the conflict in the field of social ideas. But all the same he was a bookish man, and gave no impression of having a passionate nature. He wrote novels with a moral purpose, but he possessed no special talent for literature. Notwithstanding the breadth of his learning, Chernishevsky was not a man of high culture. His standard of culture was rather low compared with that of the people of the 'forties. There was a lack of taste in it, due to the influence of the seminarists and *raznochintsi.*

Chernishevsky was a rationalist, a disciple of Feuerbach and at the same time one who idealized the soil, like Dobrolyubov and like all the best representatives of the revolutionary and nihilist intelligentsia. He had a strong ascetic side to him also. It was a result of his asceticism that he professed his extreme materialism, which was, philosophically speaking, naïve and pitiful; and it was due to his moral sense and love of the good that he affirmed a utilitarian ethic of rational egoism. The ethical motive was always very strong among the nihilists, though theoretically they repudiated all morals. Idealism, spiritual metaphysics, and religion were connected in their minds with practical materialism and social injustice. Christianity provided sufficient grounds for this. Those who professed to have an idealistic and spiritual outlook too often concealed the basest self-interest behind the expression of lofty ideas. And, therefore, on behalf of a vital idealism, for the sake of the realization of social justice, they began to assert a crude materialism and utilitarianism, and to reject all lofty ideas and rhetoric.

Chernishevsky wrote a utopian novel called *What is to be done?* which became a sort of catechism of Russian nihilism, a text-book of the Russian revolutionary intelligentsia. From an artistic point of view the novel was sufficiently weak and tasteless, but it is very interesting from the point of view of the history of the Russian intelligentsia. The attacks upon it on moral grounds from the right wing were monstrously unjust and libellously false. The notable Russian theologian, Bukharev, who recognized its Christian character, was right. *What is to be done?* is an ascetic book, a sort of manual of the devout life for Russian nihilists. Rakhmetov, the hero, sleeps on nails in order to harden his character and train himself to endure pain and suffering. The preaching of free love did not mean the preaching of dissoluteness, a thing which flourished precisely among the conservative governing classes, the guards officers and so on, but not among the nihilists, who were men of ideas. It meant a demand for sincerity in emotion, a liberation from all conventions, lies and oppression. Chernishevsky's ethics, of course, stood a great deal higher than the slave morality of 'Domostroi'. Vera Pavlovna's dream in the novel pictures a socialist Utopia in which co-operative workshops are organized. Chernishevsky's socialism, more than any other, still bore a partly *narodnik* and partly utopian character, but was already one of the predecessors of the Communism of the 'sixties. Plekhanov, the founder of Russian Marxism, recognizes this in his book on Chernishevsky.(12) Not without reason did Marx study Russian in order to read Chernishevsky.

It was as an economist that the latter was most independent. He was not, like many other *narodniks*, an opponent of industrial development. But he poses the traditional problem for Russian nineteenth century thought: Can Russia escape capitalist development? and answers it by saying that Russia can shorten the capitalist period to nothing, and go straight on from the lower forms of economy to socialist economy. The communists, in spite of their Marxism, are trying to do just this very thing. Chernishevsky sets national wealth and popular well-being in opposition to each other, which was characteristic of *narodnik* socialism. In capitalist countries, national wealth increases and the people's welfare diminishes. Chernishevsky is a defender of the peasant Commune. He asserts that the third and highest socialist period of development will resemble the first and lowest. Chernishevsky, like Hertzen and later Mikhailovsky, identifies the interests of the people with the interests of human personality in general. Of all those who wrote books that the law allowed to be published, Chernishevsky was the most clearly expressed socialist, and this marks his significance for the Russian intelligentsia, which in its moral consciousness was most wholly socialist in the second half of the nineteenth century. Nihilism of the Pisarev type was a weakening of the socialist theme, but this was a temporary phenomenon. Chernishevsky's philosophical position was specially weak. Although he derived it from so admirable a thinker as Feuerbach, yet his materialism was vulgar, and coloured by the popular natural science books of that day, much more vulgar than the dialectic materialism of the Marxists.

Chernishevsky wrote on æsthetic questions too, and was a typical representative of Russian journalistic criticism. He defended the thesis that reality is higher than art and desired to construct a realist æsthetic. There was a strong ascetic motive in Chernishevsky's anti-æstheticism. He was already seeking that type of culture which triumphed in communism—frequently in caricature—the dominance of the natural and economic sciences, the rejection of religion and metaphysics, the subservience of literature and art to social aims, an ethic of social utilitarianism, the subjection of the internal life of the individual to the interests and requirements of society. Chernishevsky's asceticism and the practical Christian virtues of this 'materialist' provided an immense endowment of moral capital on which the communists are living, although they themselves do not possess those virtues.

In contrast with Chernishevsky and Dobrolyubov, Pisarev, the principal exponent of Russian nihilism in the proper sense, was a scion of the nobility. He was an elegant and smart young man with gentle, by no means nihilist, manners. This 'destroyer of æsthetics' had æsthetic taste. As a writer he was more gifted than Chernishevsky and Dobrolyubov. His fate was typically Russian. He was arrested on some trivial ground and spent four years in prison in solitary confinement, where he wrote most of his essays. Pisarev died soon after he was set free, and when he was quite a young man, being drowned as a result of an unfortunate accident. Coming from a generation of prophets of enlightenment in the 'sixties, he was very much of an individualist, and the social theme was weaker in him than in Chernishevsky. Pisarev was mainly interested in the emancipation of the individual person, in its liberation from superstition and prejudice, from the ties of family, from traditional morals, and the conventions of life. Intellectual freedom held a central position for him, and he hoped to attain it by popularizing natural science. He preached materialism, which he was naïvely convinced sets personality free, although at the same time materialism denies personality. If personality is entirely produced by environment, then it cannot possess freedom and independence of any sort.

Pisarev wanted to produce a new type of human being; this interested him more than the organization of society. This new human type he called 'the thinking realist'. The realist generation of 'sons' is sharply opposed to the idealist generation of 'fathers'. In his type of 'thinking realist' Pisarev anticipated to a large extent the type produced by Russian communism. A number of the traits of this 'thinking realist' were sketched by Turgeniev in Bozarov (*Fathers and Sons*), though not with any particular success. Among the Russian intelligentsia, before the appearance of nihilism, the human type predominated which was known as the 'idealist of the 'forties'. It was the continuation of the type which belonged to the end of the eighteenth and beginning of the nineteenth centuries, and was connected with mystical masonry. It was the outcome of the working over by Russian thought of German romanticism and idealism. It grew up on the soil provided by cultured Russian gentry. This type of man, a very honourable type, was prone to the highest aspirations, to appreciation of taste and beauty. As later on Dostoyevsky loved to observe with irony, it was given to much day dreaming and had but a feeble capacity for action and putting into practice; there was no little of the Russian laziness to which the gentry were liable. From this type the 'superfluous people' came. The type of 'thinking realist' preached by Pisarev produces completely different traits, which are often engendered in reaction against the idealist type. The 'thinking realist' was alien from all day dreaming and romanticism; he was the foe of all lofty ideas which had no relation whatever to action and were not put into practice. He was inclined to be cynical when it came to unmasking illusions, whether religious, metaphysical or æsthetic. His cult was a cult of work and labour. He recognized only the natural sciences, and despised the humanities. He preached the ethic of reasoned egoism, not because he was more egoistic than the idealist type (on the contrary, the reverse was the case), but because he desired the merciless exposure of fraudulent lofty ideas which were made to subserve the basest interests.

But the level of philosophical culture of the 'thinking realists' was low, much lower than that of the 'idealists of the 'forties'. Buchner and Moleshott—exponents of the most vulgar materialism based on the popularization of the natural science of the day—were taken to be notable philosophers and became teachers. This was a terrible fall from Feuerbach, not to speak of Hegel. The 'thinking realists' set out to find the solution of the mystery of life and of existence in the dissection of a frog. It was precisely from the 'thinking realists' of the 'sixties that there came that absurd argument, which became so popular among the radical Russian intelligentsia, that the dissection of a corpse did not reveal the existence of a soul in man. The reverse bearing of this argument escaped their notice; if they had brought the soul to light by the dissecting of a corpse, this would have been evidence on the side of materialism. There was a great contrast between the seriousness and significance of the human crisis which took place in the 'thinking realists', and the pitifulness of their philosophy, their crude and vulgar materialism and utilitarianism.

The 'thinking realist' was, of course, a foe of æsthetics, and denied the independent significance of art. In that respect he demanded a stern asceticism. Pisarev perpetrated a positive pogrom of æsthetics; he rejected the perfect achievement of Pushkin, and proposed that the Russian novelists should write popular tracts on natural science. In this respect the cultural programme of the communists is more reasonable; it proposes the study of Pushkin, and assigns some meaning to art. Dialectic materialism is less vulgar than the materialism of Buchner and Moleshott. But among the communists technical knowledge plays the same part as natural science, and especially the biological sciences, played in the 'sixties. Pisarev's nihilism announced that 'boots are above Shakespeare'. The idea of the subservience of art and literature to social aims was asserted in Pisarev's system in an even more extreme form than in communism. If the programme of Russian nihilism were actually realised to the full in Russian communism, the results for culture would have been more destructive than those we actually see in Soviet culture. The appearance of the 'thinking realist' meant the appearance of a harsher type than the 'idealist of the 'forties', and at the same time a more active type. But in the nihilism of Pisarev there was a healthy reaction against fruitless, romantic day dreaming, idleness and egoistic self-absorption; it was a wholesome summons to labour and knowledge, although a one-sided knowledge. There was a simple and active liberating force in nihilism. The movement had an immense and a positive significance for the emancipation of women. An analogous process recurred among us Russians in the change from the type of person who created the cultural renaissance of the beginning of the twentieth century—the 'idealist' movement of that day—to the Russian communist.

The exponents of nihilism did not observe the radical contradiction which lay at the roots of their aspirations. They sought the liberation of personality; they proclaimed a revolt against all beliefs, all abstract ideas, for the sake of that liberation. On behalf of the liberation of personality, they emptied it of its qualitative content, devastated its inner life, and denied it its right to creativeness and spiritual enrichment. The principle of utilitarianism is in the highest degree unfavourable to the principle of personality; it subjects personality to utility, which holds sway tyrannically over personality. In its thought and creative activity nihilism displayed a violent asceticism intruded from without. Materialism was such an intruded asceticism and poverty of thought. The principle of personality can in no way stand and develop on the soil of materialism. Personality, as they conceived it, is found to be deprived of the right to creative fulness of life. If the talented Pisarev had lived to more mature years, he would perhaps have observed this fundamental contradiction; perhaps he would have understood that one cannot fight for personality on the ground of one's belief 'in the frog'. The tendencies of the 'seventies rubbed off the corners of the nihilism of the 'sixties. The chief influence on the thought of the radical intelligentsia of the 'seventies was not that of Buchner and Moleshott, but of Comte and Herbert Spencer. A change-over took place from materialism to positivism, a reaction against the predominance of natural science. To some extent the rights of æsthetics were upheld, and art was not repudiated. But the idea of the subservience of art to social aims continued to dominate the minds of the intelligentsia.

CHAPTER III
RUSSIAN *NARODNICHESTVO* AND ANARCHISM

Narodnichestvo is a phenomenon just as characteristically Russian as nihilism or anarchism. The Slavophils and Hertzen, Dostoyevsky and Bakunin, L. Tolstoi and the revolutionaries of the 'seventies were all alike *narodniks*, though in different ways. *Narodnichestvo* is above all belief in the Russian people, and by the people must be understood the simple labouring people, and especially the peasantry. The people are not the nation. Russian *narodniks* of all shades believed that among the people was preserved the secret of the true life, a secret concealed from the governing cultured classes. Consciousness of the gulf between the intelligentsia and the people was fundamental to *narodnichestvo*. The *narodniks* of the intelligentsia did not feel themselves an organic part of the people; the people was to be found outside them. Intelligentsia was not a function of the life of the people, it was broken off from that life, and felt guilty in relation to the people.

This sense of guilt played an immense part in the psychology of *narodnichestvo*. The intelligentsia was always in debt to the people, and had to pay its debt. All the culture which the intelligentsia accepted was built up at the people's expense, at the expense of the people's labour, and this laid a heavy responsibility upon those who shared in that culture. The religious *narodniks* (the Slavophils, Dostoyevsky, Tolstoi) believed that in the people religious truth was hidden; those who were not religious and often anti-religious (Hertzen, Bakunin, the *narodnik* socialists of the 'seventies) believed that in the people was hidden social truth. The true man, the man who is not crushed by the sense of guilt, by the sin of ex-

[58]

ploiting his brothers, is the labouring man, the man of the people. Culture for its own sake is not a justification of life, but is bought at the too heavy price of the enslavement of the people. *Narodnichestvo* was not infrequently hostile to culture, and in any case rebelled against too great a respect for it. The *narodnichestvo* of the Slavophil religious type saw the chief guilt of the cultured upper classes in their divorce from the religious beliefs of the people, and from the people's life. *Narodnichestvo* of the socialist type had a much greater significance, for it saw the guilt of the cultured classes in this, that the whole of their life and culture was founded upon exploitation of the people's labour.

The intellectual, cultured class in Russia had but a feeble sense of their own worth and their own cultural vocation. On the heights of its creative path, the Russian genius was keenly aware of its loneliness, its separation from the soil, its guilt, and cast itself down in order to stoop into contact with the soil and the people. Such were Tolstoi and Dostoyevsky. What a difference there is in this respect between Tolstoi and Nietzsche! The general outlook on life of *narodnichestvo* has a flavour of the soil—it depends on the land. The people live under the power of the land, says that remarkable *narodnik* writer Gleb Uspensky. The *narodnik* of the intelligentsia, on the other hand, has broken away from the land, and desires to return to it. The *narodnik* view of things held good only in a peasant, agricultural country. The general outlook of the people is collective, not individual. The people are a collective whole and with it the intelligentsia desires to unite, entering into its life.

Russian *narodnichestvo* is the offspring of the cleavage of the Petrine epoch. It is a product of the consciousness of the intelligentsia that their own life could not be justified, that it was absurd, a product of the inorganic character of the ordering of Russian life as a whole. Not a single people of the West has gone through such a sense of repentance as the Russians, as represented by their privileged classes. The singular type of the 'contrite noble' came into being. He was conscious of his social, but not of his individual sin, the sin of his social position, and he repented of it. N. Mikhailovsky,

[59]

the *narodnik* sociologist of the 'seventies, distinguished between the work of conscience and the work of honour. The work of conscience goes on among the privileged classes, the nobility, while the work of honour, the demand for the recognition of human worth, goes on among the people, the lower, the oppressed classes. The upper class *narodniks* were moved especially by motives of conscience, the lower class *narodniks* by motives of honour. An aversion for the bourgeoisie and a dread of the development of capitalism have always been distinctive of the Russian people. The *narodniks* believed in a path of development for Russia, in the possibility of escaping Western capitalism; they believed that the Russian people are predestined to solve the social problem better and more quickly than the West. The revolutionary *narodniks* agreed with the Slavophils in this. The belief derives from Hertzen. One of the chief supports of *narodnik* socialism was the fact that the Roman conception of property was always alien to the Russian people. The absolute nature of private property was always denied. To the Russian mind what was important was not one's attitude to the principle of property, but one's attitude to the living man. And that, of course, was the Christian position.

It is important too to note that the Russian intelligentsia was distinguished from the Western 'intellectuals' not only spiritually but also in its social position. Western intellectuals are, socially speaking, bourgeois; objectively they belong to the privileged well-to-do class. This is due to the conditions of higher education in the West. The Russian intelligentsia was commonly proletarian, not bourgeois in the social sense of the word. After the 'sixties, even when the intelligentsia remained upper class, it was in the majority of cases an impoverished proletarianized upper class. The intelligentsia of the lower class had no means of subsistence and earned their living by giving cheap lessons, or by writing, and they were obliged to live from hand to mouth. University education in Russia was to a much less extent a privilege of the rich than in the West. This partly explains the sympathy of the Russian intelligentsia for socialism, the non-bourgeois character of its ideology. But the socialism of the intelligentsia of the nineteenth century was of a visionary character. Nowhere in the West did there exist so singular a form of the problem 'intelligentsia and people', to which all Russian thought of the second half of the nineteenth century was devoted, for in the West there existed neither intelligentsia nor people in the Russian sense. All the *narodniks* idealized the peasant way of living; the peasant Commune seemed to them an original product of Russian history, the ideal type, or, as N. Mikhailovsky expressed it, the highest type on a low rung of development. But one must not attach too great importance to the *narodnik* doctrine of the Commune; it was only the reflexion of Russian conditions of life. Great significance belongs to the moral and spiritual aspect of *narodnichestvo*. Russian communism holds a doctrine which contradicts *narodnichestvo*, but into it powerful elements of Russian revolutionary *narodnichestvo* have entered.

The beginning of the 'sixties was the period of liberal reforms, of the liberation of the peasants, the foundation of the Zemstvo. Several years of great harmony ensued because the left intelligentsia became reconciled with authority and willing to take part in the realization of reforms which originated from above. Hertzen and even Chernishevsky write laudatory essays on the peasant reforms of Alexander II and are ready to support the government in this matter. The dream of the intelligentsia of the freedom of the peasants was coming true. But this spring-like temper lasted but a short while. A reactionary mood from above and a revolutionary temper from below began to grow, and the atmosphere became more and more tense. At court, and among the nobility who suffered from the liberation of the peasants, a reactionary temper hostile to reforms soon made its appearance. The usual repressive tendency in relation to the intelligentsia won the victory. A feeling of terror began to predominate in the governing classes, as indeed it always has predominated among Russian authorities in consequence of the cleavage in Russian life and the inorganic character of the Russian State. A revolutionary movement began which found expression in terrorist acts against Alexander II. The reactionary temper of the governing classes was stimulated both by their interests and by their passions, and it found vent in acts of repression which, in their turn, aroused revolutionary temper and activity. A vicious circle was set up.

Revolutionary acts could not change the order of society, for the immense bulk of the people still believed in the sacrosanct character of the autocracy. The intelligentsia had not sufficient grasp of the fact that it was impossible for the Russian monarchy to maintain its position by mere violence, and that it rested upon the religious convictions of the people. The peasants were liberated and given land. Those who demanded the liberation of the peasants without providing them with land, that is to say, the turning of them into a proletariat, had clearly been defeated. But the peasants, in spite of the fact that they possessed the larger part of the land, remained unorganized and discontented. The level of agricultural skill was low and at a primitive stage, and the peasants had not sufficient land for their subsistence. A class regime still remained, and the peasant, as a man, continued to be humiliated. Russia was still an aristocratic country, and feudalism was not entirely superseded until the actual revolution of 1917. The great magnates who possessed immense estates still remained. Manners and morals were feudal. Notwithstanding the immense significance of the reform, everybody was discontented. After the liberation of the peasants, revolutionary *narodnichestvo*, i.e. agrarian socialism, was directed to new ends. The development of capitalist industry on a small scale began in Russia. The bourgeoisie began to grow. The prosperous peasantry in the villages was changed into the bourgeoisie. The question whether Russia could escape the capitalist stage became more acute.

In connection with the extreme maximalist tendencies of the end of the 'sixties the sinister, grim, and characteristically Russian figure of Nechaev is of particular interest. He was the founder of the revolutionary society called 'The Axe or the People's Justice'. Nechaev composed the 'Revolutionary Catechism', a document of unusual interest, unique of its kind. In this document is to be found the extreme expression of the principles of atheistic revolutionary asceticism. They are the rules by which the genuine revolutionary should be guided, his manual, as it were, of the spiritual life. Nechaev's catechism is reminiscent to a grim degree of Orthodox asceticism turned inside out and mixed with Jesuitism. He was a sort of Isaac the Syrian and Ignatius Loyola of revolutionary socialism, the extremist form of the revolutionary ascetic denial of the world. Nechaev was, of course, absolutely sincere, and his fanaticism was of the extremest kind. His was the psychology of the sectarian. He was prepared to burn his neighbour, but he was ready at any moment to be burned himself. Nechaev alarmed everybody. Revolutionaries and socialists of all shades rejected him and found that he was compromising the work of revolution and socialism. Even Bakunin repudiated Nechaev.

Nechaev and his work inspired Dostoyevsky's *The Possessed.* The affair of the murder of the student Ivanov by followers of Nechaev on the suspicion that he was an *agent provocateur* struck the imagination of Dostoyevsky and he described it in the murder of Shatov. Peter Verkhovensky, of course, bears little resemblance to Nechaev and gives one the impression of a caricature, but psychologically Dostoyevsky revealed a great deal of truth. There is something mystical in Nechaev's catechism. It is of special interest to us that Nechaev to a large extent anticipated the bolshevik type of party organization, in which everything comes from above, the extreme of centralized and despotic organization. Nechaev desired to cover the whole of Russia with those small revolutionary cells, with an iron discipline for which everything would be permissible for the sake of achieving the revolutionary purpose. Nechaev despised the masses and wanted to drag them forcibly to revolution. He rejected democracy. How does Nechaev characterize the revolutionary? 'The revolutionary is the doomed man. He has no personal interests, business, feelings, connections, property, or even name. Everything in him is in the grip of the one exclusive interest, one thought, one passion, revolution.' (13) The revolutionary has broken with civil order, with the civilized world, and with the morals of the world. He lives in this world in order to destroy it. He must not even love the sciences of this world. He knows one science only, the science of destruction. To the revolutionary everything is moral which serves the revolution —words which Lenin repeated later. The revolutionary destroys everything which hinders the attainment of his purpose. He is no revolutionary who holds anything in this world dear. The revolutionary should penetrate even the secret police and have his agents everywhere. It is necessary to increase suffering and violence in order to arouse the masses to rebellion. He must associate with outlaws, who are the real revolutionaries. He must focus this world into one invincible destructive force.

According to Nechaev the psychology of the revolutionary requires the rejection of the world and personal life, exceptional efficiency, exceptional concentration upon the one thing needful, readiness to face the pain and suffering which he must expect. This psychology is mysterious in this respect, that in it there is no belief in the help of God's grace and eternal life, as there is in Christianity. Many Christian self-denying virtues are required of the revolutionary, though for a different purpose. The great distinction from Christianity lies in this, that Christianity does not demand falsehood for the realization of its highest end, nor does it permit the use of any and every, even criminal, means. Something of Nechaev's asceticism passed over into Dzerzhinsky, the founder and controller of the Cheka. Dzerzhinsky was, of course, a fanatical believer who sanctioned every means in order to bring socialism into being. He was the cause of appalling suffering; he was covered with blood; but he himself was ready for sacrifice and suffering; he was in penal servitude for fifteen years. In his boyhood and youth he was a believing Roman Catholic and prepared for the priesthood; he switched over his energies, as did so many revolutionaries. Although the communists softened down Nechaev's catechism, a great deal from it entered into Russian communism, especially in its first period.

At the present time the communists form a state; they are occupied in construction, not destruction, and on that account are changing a good deal; they are ceasing to be typical revolutionaries. For them also there exists no neighbour, but only the man far off. For them also the world is divided into two camps, and so far as the enemy camp is concerned everything is permissible.

Nechaev himself spent ten years in the convict prison of Alexeevsky Vavelin in horrible conditions. There he carried on his propaganda. He turned the whole prison guard into his agents and through them corresponded with the party 'Narodnaya Volya', to whom he gave advice. He was a man of exceptional strength. But the triumph of such a man could forebode nothing good.

II

Anarchism is as much a characteristic child of the Russian spirit as nihilism and *narodnichestvo*. It is one of the poles in the spiritual make-up of the Russian people. The Russians are a State-minded people, submissively giving themselves to be the material for founding a great empire, and yet at the same time inclined to revolt, to turbulence, to anarchy. The Russian dionysiac element is anarchic. Stenka Razin and Pugachev were characteristically Russian figures and the memory of them is preserved among the people. The anarchist element is very strong in Russian nineteenth century thought. None of the Russian intelligentsia liked the State and they did not consider that it was theirs. The State was 'They', 'The others'. 'We' lived on a different level, alien from every State. If the idea of the sacred anointing of authority was characteristic of the Russian, so also was the idea that all authority is evil and sinful. We have seen that the basis which the Slavophils gave to autocratic monarchy included a powerful anarchist element. Constantine Aksakov was a real anarchist. There are passages in him which recall Bakunin. And there is a strong anarchist element in Dostoyevsky also. The Russian *narodniks* did not grasp the significance of the State nor consider the question how to obtain power in the State. Yaroslavsky reproaches them on this account in his *History of the Communist Party*. (14) The ideal future was always represented as stateless. The State is the hateful present.

The most amazing thing of all is that the ideology of anarchism is for the most part the creation of the highest circle of the Russian landed gentry, and this Russian anarchism acquired a general European importance. Bakunin, Prince Kropotkin, Count Tolstoi, *grands seigneurs* all of them, these were the founders of Russian and world anarchism. The central figure is Bakunin, who was the fantastic child of the Russian gentry. He was an overgrown child, always aflame with the most extreme revolutionary ideas, a Russian visionary, incapable of methodical thought and discipline, something in the nature of a Stenka Razin of the Russian gentry. He was still a man of the 'forties, a friend of Belinsky, Hertzen, the Slavophils, at that time an idealist and a Hegelian, but in the 'sixties and especially in the 'seventies he acquired importance, and that a European importance. He quarrelled with Marx about the First International, into which he wanted to introduce anarchist principles, decentralization and federalism. At first Bakunin was on good personal terms with Marx, upon whom he even had some influence in his teaching about the messianic vocation of the proletariat. (15) But later on he became Marx's mortal enemy, regarding him as an apostle of the State and a pan-Germanist. Bakunin did not like the Germans; he preferred the Latin peoples, and his principal book is called *The Cat-o'-Nine-Tails German Empire and the Social Revolution.*

There was a very strong Slavophil element in Bakunin. His revolutionary messianism is Russian-Slav. He believed that the world-wide conflagration would be kindled by the Russian people and Slavdom. And in this Russian revolutionary messianism he is a forerunner of communism. The saying 'the passion for destruction is a creative passion' is Bakunin's. Bakunin's anarchism is insurrection; he wants to raise a world-wide revolt; he wants to destroy the old world; he believes that on the ruins of the old world, from the ashes of the old, the new world will spontaneously arise. Bakunin wants to raise the proletarian masses of the whole world in rebellion; he would turn to the rabble, the lowest classes, and believes that the insurgent mob, throwing off all the fetters of history and civilization, will establish a better and a free life; he wants to unshackle the mob. Bakunin was a *narodnik* in the sense that he believed in truth hidden in the labouring people, in the unenlightened masses, and especially in the Russian people, whom he regarded as pre-eminently a rebel people. All evil lies in the State, which was founded by the ruling classes and is an instrument of oppression.

Marx was intellectual; he ascribed an immense importance to theory, philosophy, science; he did not believe in the type of politics which is based on the emotions; he ascribed enormous importance to the development of thought and organization. Bakunin was exceptionally emotional, and hostile to all intellectual theories; he thoroughly disapproved of scholars and scholarship. Above all, it was the authority of the learned that he hated. To him scientific socialism meant that the pundits were in power. We must not allow science to control life; we must give authority to no one. He idealized the outlaw Razin-Pugachev element in the Russian people. At the outset of the revolution the bolsheviks made great use of this element in spite of their Marxist theories. Lavrov, one of the exponents of the revolutionary socialist movement of the 'seventies, wanted to educate the people and expected the revolution to follow this education. Bakunin wanted to raise the people in revolt, without educating them, he believed in the righteousness and power of the unorganized. To Bakunin light will flare up from the East and enlighten the darkness of the West, the darkness of the bourgeois world. The Russian communists also will come to the same view in spite of their Western Marxism.

To Bakunin, man becomes man by revolt. There are three principles of human development: (1) the animal man, (2) thought, (3) revolt. Bakunin sets revolt over against organization. To him Marx was a Jacobin and he could not bear Robespierre and the Jacobins. Bakunin was a communist, but his communism was anti-State and anarchist. He believed in the Union of Producing Associations. Bakunin was convinced that the Slavs, left to themselves, would not have founded a State, and upon this was based his belief in the mission of Slavism. To Bakunin the State represents above all German influence. He predicted that if in any country Marxism should come into being it would be a terrible tyranny. Some of Bakunin's predictions sound prophetic now.

But Bakunin's atheism was even more militant, crude and violent that Marx's atheism; it was due to his passionate maximalist Russian temperament. Marx was a man of thought. To him the conflict with religion was above all a question of change of thought. Bakunin was an emotional man and his atheism gives the impression not of a rejection of the idea of God as untrue and harmful, but of a fight against God. There is something of Marcion's ideas in his atheism. One of his principal writings is called *God and the State*. To Bakunin the State was the source of all the evil in world history, and meant the enslavement and captivity of man; but belief in God was the chief support of the State. All authority is of God. To Bakunin that means that all authority is of the devil; to him God is the devil, the source of man's authority over man, the cause of enslavement and violence, 'If there is a God, then man is a slave.' The idea of God is the denial of human reason, of justice and of freedom. God is the avenger. All religions are cruel. It is, in fact, a materialism which is idealist in practice. In religion, the divine is lifted up into heaven and what is crudely animal remains on the earth. This is Feuerbach's thought, reiterated later on by Marx.

Bakunin, in contrast with Belinsky, spoke very harshly about Christ. Christ ought to have been shut up in prison as an idler and a tramp. If man is endowed with an immortal soul and with freedom, then he is an anti-social being. (16) For an immortal soul does not need the community. The community gives birth to the individual; the community is the source of morals. In contrast with Max Stirner, Bakunin's anarchism is anti-individual, collective, communist. Bakunin repudiated personality and its independent worth and autonomy; this distinguishes him from Proudhon. He preached an anarchist communism; but as distinct from the anarchist communism of Kropotkin, which was tinged with intellectual optimism, Bakunin's was tinged with a sinister shade of destructiveness and revolt against everything, and especially against God. Bakunin associated churches and public-houses to-

[68]

gether; he cried: 'The social revolution alone will be able to acquire sufficient strength to close all the public-houses and all the churches at one and the same time.' (17) Bakunin's militant atheism goes further than that of the Russian communists who, as a matter of fact, have not closed all the churches and in whom the intellectual influence of Marxism can be felt; but in his militant atheism Bakunin is a predecessor of the communists. Communism has made great use of his anarchism and spirit of rebellion in the destructive side of its work, but on the creative and constructive side, and in their organization, the communists are sharply distinguished from Bakunin, who never could organize power and had no wish to do so. Bakunin, like Nechaev, was hostile to science and the intelligentsia, and this aversion also played its part in the Russian revolution.

In comparison with the extremes of Bakunin and Nechaev, the other currents of Russian revolutionary socialist thought were mild and moderate. In philosophy they took the form of positivism, under the influence of Comte, Mill and Spencer, and even of the rising neo-Kantianism, but not of militant materialism. A crude utilitarianism in morals was predominant and, in general, extreme nihilism. In social teaching many of them came near to Proudhon, and borrowed something from Marx, with whom they were beginning to be acquainted. The master minds among the intelligentsia of the 'seventies were P. Lavrov and N. Mikhailovsky, the defenders of what was called subjective sociology, that is to say, the point of view which sees it is necessary for sociology to assign moral value to phenomena. Lavrov and Mikhailovsky in their own way defended human personality without distinguishing it from the individual, and socialism to them, as to Hertzen, has an individualist character. The socialist organization of society is necessary to ensure a complete life for each individual. Mikhailovsky declared 'war for individuality' and set up a theory of a conflict between personality and organized society.

Lavrov and Mikhailovsky are typical armchair philosophers of the radical intelligentsia. The weakness of their philosophic position, their superficial positivism, prevented them from giving a philosophic basis to the principle of personality, which was the positive side of their sociological theory. To them personality still remained the creation of the community, of its social environment, and it is not clear whence it found its power to fight against the community, which wants to turn personality into its own organ and function. Lavrov became known through his *Historical Letters,* which became the moral catechism of the *narodnik* intelligentsia of the 'seventies. Lavrov gave expression to the theme of 'repentance', of the guilt of the cultured classes before the masses and of their obligation to discharge their debt. He poses the traditional Russian question of the price of progress and culture. But the *narodnichestvo* of Lavrov and Mikhailovsky belongs to the type which regards itself as bound by the interests of the people but not by their opinions. They thought that true enlightened opinions are to be found among the intelligentsia and not among the people. It was the duty of the intelligentsia to give the people knowledge, to serve the interests of the people and work for their freedom, but to preserve its own independence in opinions and ideas. Mikhailovsky put this in the following way: 'If the revolutionary masses broke into my room and wanted to smash the bust of Belinsky and destroy my library, I should resist them to the last drop of blood.' There, as it were, he foresaw the situation in which the radical intelligentsia were to find themselves placed in their struggle for revolution. Mikhailovsky less than anybody, of course can be regarded as a forerunner of communism, much less so than Belinsky and Bakunin, and in this respect he is like Hertzen. This was another streak in Russian socialist thought. The revolutionary masses will desire to smash the bust of Belinsky precisely because they will be imbued with some of that same Belinsky's ideas. Therein lies the paradox of revolutionary thought.

In the 'seventies there was a strong *narodnik* movement which found expression in the 'going to the people'. This movement did not at first bear a revolutionary and political character. The *narodniks* of the intelligentsia desired to merge themselves into the people, to enlighten the people, to serve the peasants in their daily needs and interests. They wanted 'land and liberty' for the people, and with this was connected the underground organization called 'Land and Liberty'. The failure of this 'going to the people', in which so much self-denial and capacity for sacrifice, so much faith and hope, so much nobility were displayed, was, of course, due to the fact that they came up against government repression and persecution, but not only to that. The tragedy of the *narodnik* movement lay above all in this, that the people did not welcome the intelligentsia, and the people themselves surrendered those who came desiring to serve them so unselfishly and disinterestedly into the hands of the authorities. The people—that is to say, chiefly the peasantry—found the point of view of the intelligentsia strange. The people still remained religious, Orthodox, and the lack of religion in the intelligentsia repelled them. The people saw a gentlefolk's pastime in the *narodnik* 'going to the people'. All this brought the *narodnik* intelligentsia face to face with a political problem and led to the elaboration of new methods of conflict.

III

In the 'seventies a notable exponent of the theory of revolution was P. N. Tkachev.(18) He, more than anyone, should be regarded as the forerunner of Lenin. Tkachev edited a revolutionary paper abroad, called *The Tocsin*, which expressed the most extreme views. Tkachev, by the way, was the first during the 'seventies to talk to us about Marx. In 1875, he wrote a letter to Engels about Russia's own particular line of development and about the special character of the coming Russian revolution, to which it would be impossible simply to apply the principles of Marxism. But it cannot be said that Tkachev set *narodnik* principles in opposition to the idea of transplanting Marxism to Russian soil. Tkachev was not a traditional and typical *narodnik*; as a matter of fact he did not believe in the people. He was the first to draw the distinction between a bourgeois revolution, a constitution, etc., and that Russian application of Marxism which considers the development of capitalism necessary in Russia—a point of view very much akin to Russian bolshevism. There the divergence between Lenin and Plekhanov is already to be noted.

Tkachev has no desire to allow Russia to be transformed into a constitutional and bourgeois state. He considers that the absence of a developed bourgeoisie is Russia's greatest advantage, as facilitating the possibility of a social revolution. The Russian people are socialist by instinct. Tkachev was not a democrat; he affirmed the authority of the minority over the majority. Tkachev was called a Jacobin, but that is not entirely true. Jacobinism is a form of democracy, while Tkachev is above all a socialist and his socialism is not of the democratic sort, in which respect he is like Lenin and the communists. Tkachev was an opponent of the *narodnik* movements, 'Land and Liberty' and the 'Black Redistribution', which rejected the idea of a purely political conflict. His relation to these currents of thought was very reminiscent of Lenin's attitude towards what are called 'The Economists', who placed before the working classes purely economic proposals, leaving the political conflict to a large extent to liberal tendencies. In the history of revolutionary currents of thought in Russia Tkachev is the predecessor of 'The People's Will', which, as distinct from the *narodnik* movements of the 'seventies, set itself the political problem of overthrowing absolute monarchy by terrorism. 'The People's Will' represents the victory of Tkachev over Lavrov and Bakunin. Tkachev, like Lenin, was an exponent of the theory of revolution. His fundamental idea was the seizure of power by a revolutionary minority. This required the disorganization of the existing authority by terrorism. The masses in Tkachev's opinion are always ready for revolution, because they are only the material of which a revolutionary minority makes use. Revolutions are made but not prepared for. Tkachev does not recognize any sort of evolution. Revolution ought not to be preceded by propaganda and the education of the masses.

But Tkachev was definitely opposed to Bakunin's anarchism; he thinks the destruction of the State absurd; he speaks of the replacement of conservative institutions by revolutionary, almost in the same way as Lenin is to speak of it later. Bakunin's anarchist dionysism was completely alien to Tkachev. Bakunin was opposed to all organization. Tkachev was in favour of organizing a revolutionary minority which would seize power. He was one of the few Russian revolutionaries of the past, almost the only one, who thought in terms of authority, of capturing and organizing it. His desire was that the revolutionary socialist party should become a government, and in this respect he is very like Lenin. He pictured the revolutionary socialist government as sufficiently despotic; the destruction of everything belonging to the past would be even more merciless with Tkachev than with Lenin, but the time for that had not yet come, and Tkachev's ideas were not particularly popular in Russian revolutionary circles. The will to power preached by Tkachev was in sharp opposition to the temper of the Russian *narodnik* socialists.

G. V. Plekhanov, the founder of Russian Marxism and Social Democracy, was already writing decisively and sharply against Tkachev in the 'eighties. This is one of the basic themes of his book *Our Divergencies*. Plekhanòv's controversy with Tkachev is of great interest because it sounds as though Plekhanov was arguing against Lenin and the bolsheviks at a time when they did not yet exist. Plekhanov rebelled especially against the idea of a seizure of power by the revolutionary socialist party. He considered such a seizure would be the greatest misfortune, and pregnant with future reaction. Plekhanov was also opposed to Bakuninism and revolt. He was a Westernizer, a rationalist, a believer in 'enlightenment' and an evolutionist. The non-rational impulses of the Russian were alien to him; he defended science and philosophy against the revolutionary obscurantism of Bakunin and Tkachev. Plekhanov, like all the Marxist mensheviks later on, had no wish to recognize special paths of development for Russia or the possibility of a peculiarly Russian revolution, and in this he was certainly mistaken. Tkachev was more in the right. Tkachev, like Lenin, constructed a theory of socialist revolution in Russia. A Russian revolution would necessarily not follow the Western pattern. With this was connected the special problem in the history of Russian socialist thought, i.e. Can Russia escape capitalist development and the rule of the bourgeoisie? Can the revolution be socialist? Can Marxist theory be applied to Russia without taking account of any special path of development for Russia?

Tkachev was right in his opposition to Engels, and his rightness was not the rightness of *narodnichestvo* against Marxism, but the historical rightness of the bolsheviks against the mensheviks, of Lenin against Plekhanov. In Russia it was not a communist revolution which turned out to be utopian, but a liberal bourgeois revolution. Marx was not very fond of the Russians; he could not endure Bakunin; he did not like Hertzen. In his attitude to Russia the real pan-German imperialist sometimes made himself felt, but he ascribed an immense importance to Russia and the possibility of a Russian revolution. He even learned Russian and followed Russian controversies about revolution and socialism. He wrote a notable letter to N. Mikhailovsky.(19) As I have already said, he valued Chernishevsky very highly, but Marx and Engels spoke of the bourgeois character of the coming Russian revolution and were in favour of the 'People's Will' party which concentrated exclusively upon the overthrow of absolute monarchy, and in this respect they were much less the forerunners of Lenin than Tkachev was. Marx and Engels did not understand the special character of Russia's path of development and were mensheviks, however much the bolsheviks have tried to disguise this. But Tkachev was a bolshevik, as Nechaev was, and even to some extent Bakunin, though to a less degree, since he repudiated power and organization. In the 'seventies the controversies were already indicated, which the Russian Marxists and *narodniks* waged in the 'nineties, and the bolsheviks and mensheviks at the beginning of the twentieth century.

The murder of Alexander II by the decision of the 'People's Will' party was the end and the disruption of the Russian revolutionary movement before the rise of Marxism. It was the tragic climax of the single combat between Russian authority and the Russian intelligentsia. At the head of the terrorist organization 'People's Will', which was responsible for the murder of 1st March, 1881, stood the heroic figure of Zhelyabov. Zhelyabov himself came from the peasantry; and at first he was a *narodnik* and denied the importance of the political conflict. The fruitlessness of the movement of the intelligentsia towards the people led Zhelyabov to the conclusion that a fight with autocracy was inevitable, as the first matter to hand. Zhelyabov was certainly not a fanatic like Nechaev. On the contrary, he was a man marked out for the experience of the fulness and harmony of life. Least of all was he materialist, and of all the Russian revolutionaries he stood the nearest to Christianity. At his trial for the affair of 1st March, to the question, was he an Orthodox? he answered: 'I was baptized in Orthodoxy, but I repudiate it, although I acknowledge the essence of Christ's teaching. This essential teaching occupies an honoured place among my moral convictions. I believe in the truth and righteousness of that faith and I solemnly acknowledge that faith without works is dead and that every genuine Christian should fight for justice, for the rights of the oppressed and the weak and if need be, also suffer for them; that is my faith.' (20) Before his execution he kissed the Cross. His communist biographer, A. Voronsky, found this fact very disturbing. He explained Zhelyabov's sympathies with Christianity by the fact that he was a *narodnik* of the 'seventies and not of the 'sixties. I think that a great part was played in it by the fact that Zhelyabov was a man of the people; and such a man, from the purest motives, from love of truth and righteousness, was obliged to devote his life to the organization of murder. It was a dreadful tragedy of Russian life.

Zhelyabov was not in his general point of view a forerunner of Russian communism, but in his methods of organization and in his action he was. The history of Russian revolutionaries is a martyrology, and the communists have made use of this martyrology as moral capital. The Russian Government in history committed moral suicide by creating martyrs.

CHAPTER IV
RUSSIAN NINETEENTH CENTURY
LITERATURE AND ITS PREDICTIONS

I

We now pass into another world, into another spiritual atmosphere, the atmosphere of the great Russian literature of the nineteenth century. This literature is the greatest monument of the Russian spirit and acquired world-wide importance. But in relation to the origin of Russian communism, one of its characteristics is particularly important. Russian literature is the most prophetic in the world; it is full of forebodings and predictions; alarm at impending catastrophe is characteristic of it. Many Russian writers of the nineteenth century felt that Russia was hanging over an abyss and falling into it. Russian nineteenth century literature bears witness to the inward revolution which was being brought about, and to the impending outward revolution. The whole nineteenth century, of all the centuries in Russian history the greatest in creative power, was a century of growing revolution. The spirit of schism and cleavage which marked this period brought Russian creative power to its highest intensity. The Russian literature of this century did not belong to the renaissance in spirit; only in Pushkin were there some flashes of the renaissance. That was the Golden Age of Russian poetry. But that Russian renaissance was achieved within a very narrow circle of the Russian nobility; it quickly came to an end, and literature took other paths.

Beginning with Gogol, Russian literature becomes didactic. It seeks truth and righteousness, and teaches the bringing of truth into actual life. Russian literature was not born of a happy creative profusion, but of suffering and the painful fate of mankind, out of the search for salvation for all men. But this means that the fundamental themes of Russian literature were religious. It evinced a

[76]

sympathy with humanity which amazed the whole world. It was in the Russian writers that the problem of culture was stated with peculiar sharpness and the justification of culture was doubted, as in the currents of Russian social thought; and this was due to a structure of spirit produced by Orthodoxy, a spirit in which there remained a very strong ascetic element, a search for salvation, and the expectation of another higher life. Psychologically Gogol, L. Tolstoi and Dostoyevsky to a large extent joined hands with Belinsky, Bakunin, Chernishevsky, Pisarev and the *narodniks* of the 'seventies, although they were anti-materialist and their work was coloured by religion. Western people scarcely ever had any doubt about the justification of civilization; this was a purely Russian doubt and arose not among those Russians who had not yet acquired any culture but frequently among those who were to be found on its highest level. Russian writers, especially the most notable, did not believe in the stability of civilization, in the stability of those principles upon which the world rests, what was called the bourgeois world of their time; they are full of terrible forebodings of impending disaster. European literature does not know that sort of religious and social unrest, for it belongs to a civilization which is more fixed and crystallized, more formed, more self-contented and calm, more differentiated and distributed into categories. Integrality belonged more properly to the Russians, entirety, both in thought and in creative life. Russian thinkers, Russian creators, when they are of note spiritually always sought not so much a perfect culture, and perfect products of creative power, as perfect life, the perfect expression of truth in life. This accounts for the realism of Russian nineteenth century literature, which is frequently misunderstood. The great Russian literature reached a stage beyond European classicism and romanticism. It was realist, but certainly not realist in the scholastic sense of the word. It was realist in an almost religious sense and in its highest form purely religious. It was realist in the sense of revealing the truth and the depth of life. In this sphere Gogol's manner was more romantic, Tolstoi's more classic. Russian writers with unusual acuteness lived through the tragedy of creative power faced by the imperative need to transform life itself, to bring truth into actual expression. Gogol and Tolstoi were ready to sacrifice the creation of perfect literary products for the sake of creating a perfect life. Russian writers were not shackled by the conventional standards of civilization and, therefore, they touched the mystery of life and death. They passed out beyond the boundaries of art. Such were Gogol, Tolstoi and Dostoyevsky. Pushkin alone stated the problem of freedom in creative activity, and of the independence of the creative activity of the poet, its independence, that is, of 'the mob', by which he understood, of course, not the people as a whole but the nobility, officials and court society among whom he lived. Gogol had already stated the problem of the social mission of art, of the vocation of the writer to social service. He desired what in its vulgarized form Russian communism calls '*sotsialny zakaz*',[1] the subordination of art to social ends. The great Russian writers stood alone in their day in opposition to the society around them, but they were certainly not individualists on principle. In their different ways they were looking for popular, collective, catholic art. In its exposure of the injustices of existing society, in its search for truth and repentance, literature fulfilled a social mission which in accord with the Russian spiritual make-up, was with many a religious social mission.

Russian poetry was full of forebodings of coming revolution and sometimes invoked it. Pushkin was considered the singer of imperial Russia and in fact many reasons could be given for regarding him as an imperialist in his general outlook, and less of a schismatic than other Russian writers. He regarded Peter the Great with hero worship; he was inspired by the greatness of Russia; but after all his poetry had been published it became clear how much of it was revolutionary. There is a great difference between the first and the second half of his literary activity; this can be seen from the change in his attitude to Radishchev. Pushkin belonged to the generation of the Decembrists; they were his friends, but the destruction of the Decembrist movement, as it

[1]See footnote on p. 83.

were, convinced him of the might of the Russian monarchy. There were two sides to Pushkin; he had, as it were, two faces; he had a love for the greatness and might of Russia, but he had also a passionate love for freedom. He had an absolutely special love of his own freedom distinct from the Russian intelligentsia's love of it. He is the real singer of freedom.

> 'We wait, our yearning hearts are beating
> With hope of sacred liberty
> As a youthful lover waits to see
> The lagging hour of sweet heart-greeting.'

In Pushkin, as it were, two things were for a moment united which have always been separated among us—the ideology of empire and the ideology of the intelligentsia. He wrote of himself:

> 'And simple folk for long the thought of me will cherish
> Because my lyre made hearts to kindliness incline,
> And pity I invoked on those who fall and perish
> And Freedom's praises sang in this cruel age of mine.'

In *The Village* Pushkin describes the charm and poetry of the Russian countryside, but he suddenly remembers the injustice, the slavery, the darkness with which the charm of that country life is linked and that the charm exists only for the privileged minority. The poem ends with the words:

> 'Ah, shall I see, my friends, a people unafflicted?
> A Tsar sweep slavery hence among forgotten things?
> Will Freedom like a glorious dawn upon our country
> Rise at long last on her light-shedding wings?'

But specially interesting in connection with Pushkin in his revolutionary mood is the poem *Freedom*:

> 'I sing the freedom of the world
> And smite the vice on kingly thrones.'

In this poem there are terrible words about the Tsars:

> 'Thou autocrat of evil deed,
> On thee and thine my execration!

With fierce delight I yield thy seed
To death, and thee to thy damnation!'

Pushkin was aware of the rebellious element in the Russian people and foresaw the possibility 'of a Russian revolt senseless and merciless'; in Pushkin, at his most harmonious, we must not look for perfect harmony, and he is aware of the unhealthiness, the division and injustice of imperial Russia.

But a most terrible impression is produced by Lermontov's poem, *Prediction*, especially in view of its fulfilment:

> 'The day will come, for Russia that dark day
> When the Tsar's diadem will fall, and they,
> Rabble who loved him once, will love no more,
> And many will subsist on death and gore.
> Downtrodden law no shelter will provide
> For child or guiltless woman. Plague will ride
> From stinking corpses through the grief-struck land
> Where fluttering rags from cottages demand
> Help none can give. And famine's gnawing pangs
> Will grip the countryside with ruthless fangs.
> Dawn on the streams will shed a crimson light.
> And then will be revealed the Man of might
> Whom thou wilt know; and thou wilt understand
> Wherefore a shining blade is in his hand.
> Sorrow will be thy lot, grief melt thine eyes
> And he will laugh at all thy tears and sighs.'

This romantic poem written in 1830 foresees the horrors of a revolution which took place almost a century later.

The third great Russian poet, Tyutchev, had a conservative rather than a revolutionary outlook, but he felt all the time that a terrible revolution was impending upon the world; in strange contrast with his conservative Slavophil general outlook, Tyutchev felt keenly the chaotic, irrational, dark elements belonging to the night of the world. The harmony and order veneered upon the world seemed to him unstable and thin.

> 'A homeless orphan, man, bereft of power
> And naked, stands before that dread abyss,

Stands face to face in this his direful hour
With its dark emptiness: and all that quickens,
Glad things and light seem now a dream long past;
'Tis unfamiliar things, unsolved, as darkness thickens
Reveal his fated heritage at last.'

Not in nature only but also in history this violent chaotic element exists, and Tyutchev had forebodings of catastrophes in history, the triumph of the powers of chaos which will overthrow the cosmos. Tyutchev was a conservative who did not believe in the stability of conservative principles. He constructed a reactionary Utopia for the saving of the world from chaotic revolution. He imagines that Christianity can be used as a conservative power. His purely political poems are weak. Only his cosmic poems are notable.

Khomyakov, the head of the Slavophil school, was not of a prophetic nature. A powerful thinker, he was a very mediocre poet, but he has a whole group of sharply accusatory poems from which it may be seen that in spite of the Slavophil idealizing of the historic past, he suffered from the great historic sins of Russia. He believed that Russia was called to make known to the world the 'sacrament of freedom', to bestow 'the spirit of holy freedom'. Russia was 'unworthy of her election', but she was 'chosen'.

'But now alas what sins lie heavy,
Many and awful on thy soul!
Thou art black with black injustice
And slavery's yoke has branded thee
And godless flattery and baneful lying
And sloth that's shameful, life-denying,
And every hateful thing in thee I see.'

And Khomyakov summons to repentance:

'For all that cries for consolation,
For every law that we have spurned,
For sins that stain our generation,
For evil deeds our fathers learned,
For all our country's bitter passion
Pray ye with tears the while ye live.

O God of Might, of Thy compassion
May'st Thou forgive! May'st Thou forgive!'

He accuses the Russian State of yielding to the basest of temptations, a passion for material power. He welcomed the defeat of Russia in the Crimean War as a just punishment. He had no desire to see the vocation of Russia in the acquisition of political might; he demanded the actual realization of justice and in this he stood in the tradition of the intelligentsia.

It pained Gogol that Russia was in the grip of the spirit of evil and injustice, that it was full of grimacing masks and that it was difficult to find a human being in it. It would be a mistake to see a satirist in Gogol; he saw the metaphysical depth of evil, not only the social appearance of it. There is now no old Russia of Gogol's time with its social evils and injustices. There is no absolute monarchy, no serfdom, none of the old inequalities; but in a deeper sense Gogol's Russia remains in Soviet Russia too, and Soviet communist Russia is full of grimacing masks and the image of man is distorted in it. Khlestakov, Nozdrev, Chichikov are to be met with in Soviet communist Russia too. In it they deal in Dead Souls, and the sham Inspector brings fear upon everyone. Most of all, Gogol penetrated that spirit of falsehood which tortured Russia. Gogol passed through a tragic religious experience; he was crushed by the weight of the evil he perceived; he scarcely saw the good in life; nor did he see the image of man. He sought a way of escape by making life Christian, and he has recorded his search in his book *Correspondence with Friends*. The book aroused a violent protest from Belinsky, who saw in it a betrayal of human progressive freedom-loving ideals. But in *Correspondence with Friends*, Gogol understood the Christianizing of life in a very petty and narrow-minded way, in fact anti-socially, and he could be interpreted as a defender of the existing order, even of serfdom. In *Correspondence with Friends* there was much that was repellent and much that did not correspond to the depth of Gogol's own religious tragedy. It was a reflection of the inconsistency and ugliness of Russian life. There was a strong ascetic element in Gogol's nature, a characteristically Russian element, and it led him to censure his own literary work.

It was at the beginning of the twentieth century that the prophetic character of Russian poetry became most distinct; it was the poetry of decline, of the end of a whole period, and there were very decadent elements in it. Nevertheless, this poetry saw a dawn ahead. The symbolist poets felt that Russia was being swept into an abyss. At times this horrified them; at times it gave them joy, as making possible a new and better life. Symbolism was an expression of the divorce of literature from social activity, and an escape into an another world. But at the same time the Russian symbolists, V. Ivanov, A. Belii, A. Blok, suffered from loneliness; they desired an art that belonged to the whole people; they tried to conquer the decadent asceticism that had set in; they were in fact looking for the '*sotsialny zakaz*',[1] to make use of Soviet terminology. Especially prophetic were the verses on Russia by A. Blok, the greatest poet of the beginning of the century:

> 'I hear the tented foe's wild riot,
>> The Tartar's shrilling trumpet call,
> And over Russia see a quiet
>> Far-spreading fire envelop all.'

In another poem from the cycle, *The Field of Kulikov*, he writes:

> 'Miles flash by, the fields roll on,
>> Stop them! No more!!
> The frightened clouds go on and on
>> To sink in gore!'

But his feeling for Russia and his forebodings about Russia found particular expression in the amazing poem *Russia*:

> 'O Russia, Russia, poor and lowly,
>> Grey-timbered peasant homes in thee,
> The music of thy winds, are holy
>> As first-born tears of love to me.
>
> To pity thee is not within me,
>> My cross I bear till thou art healed;

[1]Subordination of art to social ends. Cf. p. 78.

[83]

Whatever Sorcerer's charm thy sin be,
    Thy devastating beauty yield!

Let him entice, let him deceive thee,
    Thou wilt not perish. Passing fair
In trouble, I shall still perceive thee,
    Thy glory, veiled, will still be there.

What then? One care the more for sorrow—
    Streams noisier for this tear they share—
Thy woods and fields will stand to-morrow,
    That broidered scarf still bind thy hair.'

Another symbolist poet, Andrei Belii, exclaims in one of his poems, 'Disperse thyself in space, O Russia, Russia mine!' The poets of that pre-revolutionary time were mystical, apocalyptic; they believed in Sophìa, in new revelations, but they did not believe in Christ. Their souls were not sheathed in steel; they were defenceless, but perhaps for that very reason they were open to influences from the future, and susceptible to the inward revolution which others did not notice.

Russian writers of the nineteenth and twentieth centuries felt themselves over an abyss; they did not live in a stable society, in a strong fixed civilization. A catastrophic outlook became characteristic of the most notable and creative Russians, for a strong stable classical culture with its dividing lines, its differentiation of spheres, with its standards and its spirit of finiteness, and its fear of infinity, is very unlikely to lead to foreboding and foresight. Culture of that sort gives armour to the soul and bars it from those influences which come from an unknown future. An eschatological structure of spirit was built up in Russia, and, facing the future, faced it with forebodings of catastrophe, and the development of a particular mystical sensitiveness. The Western spirit was too securely enclosed in its civilization. Among us the atmosphere which precedes revolution was steadily increasing. The Russia of the nineteenth and twentieth centuries was radically different from the Russia of the Muscovite period; the latter had its own style of culture; it was shackled in definite forms. The soul had not yet awakened; it had not awakened to thought, or to criticism; it had not come to the parting of the ways. The touch of the West upon the Russian spirit brought about a change, and a change in a completely different direction from the ways of Western civilization.

The influence of the West upon Russia was absolutely paradoxical; it did not graft Western criteria upon the Russian spirit. On the contrary its influence let loose violent, dionysiac, dynamic and sometimes demoniac forces. Spirits were unshackled and revealed a dynamic force unknown in the period before Peter. The limitless aspirations of the Faustian man of the West, the man who belongs to modern history, in Russia revealed themselves in an entirely peculiar way, in their own distinctive manner, and found expression in the creations of Dostoyevsky's genius. The Russia which had been inherited from the past, the Russia of the nobility of the merchant class and the shop-keepers, which the period of empire had kept in being, came into conflict with the Russia of the intelligentsia, which was revolutionary and social-revolutionary in spirit, which aspired after the infinite and sought the City which is to come. This clash let loose dynamic forces and led to explosions. At the time when in the West enlightenment and culture were establishing a sort of order in accordance with fixed standards—although, of course, a relative order—in Russia enlightenment and culture overthrew standards, obliterated boundaries and evoked a revolutionary dynamic. The condition of affairs was reflected in the works of all the Russian writers.

II

The inner revolution which was going on in Russia was reflected most of all in the creative work of Dostoyevsky; it was reflected in a different way in Tolstoi; the art of Tolstoi was not prophetic, but he was a revolution in himself. It is interesting to compare these two great Russian geniuses. The relation between the artistic element and the intellectual made a sharp contrast between them. Dostoyevsky was a dynamic artist, probably the most dynamic in the world.(21) With him everything is steeped in a molten, fiery atmosphere, everything is in violent movement, nothing is fixed or finally shaped. Dostoyevsky is a dionysiac artist; he expresses the revolutionary soul and discloses the dialectic of revolution. The prophetic element is very strong in him; he faced the future, and foresaw much in it; he foresaw the Russian revolution and disclosed the ideas which governed it. But Dostoyevsky's view as set forth in *A Writer's Diary* gives the impression of conservatism, although it is a peculiar conservatism with something of revolution in it. Tolstoi was an artist of the stable and formed life. Dostoyevsky's novels are tragedies; Tolstoi's are epics. As an artist Tolstoi was not prophetic; he did not look towards the future. Dostoyevsky's dynamism and prophecy are due to the fact that he was entirely engrossed in the human problem. The subject of his thought was man. In the art of Tolstoi (his novel is the most perfect in the world's literature) human life is immersed in cosmic life, in the rotation of cosmic life. Dostoyevsky moves in history, Tolstoi in the cosmos; but it is precisely to history and not to cosmic life that dynamism and prophecy belong.

On the other hand, in thought Tolstoi certainly was a revolutionary, one who exposed the injustices of life. He was an anarchist and a nihilist; he rebelled against history and civilization with unheard of radicalism. Man ought not to obey the laws of the world; he ought to obey the law of the great Lord of life, God. Positively, Tolstoi was opposed to communism; he did not accept violence; he was the enemy of all government and rejected the technique and rational organization of life; he believed in the divine basis of nature and life; he preached love not hate. But negatively he was a forerunner of communism; he rejected the past, the traditions of history, the old culture, Church and State; he rejected every economic and social inequality; he fulminated against the privileged ruling classes; he had no love for the cultured *élite*. In Russian *narodnichestvo* of the 'seventies no small part was played by 'the conscience-stricken noble'. But it was in the creative genius of Tolstoi that the repentance of the ruling classes reached its greatest intensity. Tolstoi was entirely permeated with the thought that the life of civilized society is built up upon lies and injustice. He wished to break with that society completely. In this he was a revolutionary, but he rejected revolutionary violence. Dostoyevsky also was a revolutionary in spite of the conservative appearance of many of his views. He disliked and chided the revolutionary intelligentsia, especially because he foresaw the denial of freedom of the spirit as the final result of the ideas of a revolution which was based upon godlessness. To Dostoyevsky godlessness inevitably leads to the denial of the freedom of the spirit; this is clearly seen in that display of dialectic genius, *The Legend of the Grand Inquisitor*, and in Ivan Karamazov. Herein lies the whole originality of the charge which Dostoyevsky brings against the revolutionary intelligentsia. In making these charges he defends the freedom of the spirit, which in Dostoyevsky is entirely revolutionary and overthrows the Grand Inquisitor in every Church and State. In *The Possessed* he is seen as the prophet of the Russian revolution; he foresaw a great deal, but he was often unfair.

Dostoyevsky was a revolutionary of the spirit; he wanted revolution, but revolution with God and Christ. He was the enemy of atheistic socialism, which to him was another aspect of the lure of the Grand Inquisitor and a surrender of the freedom of the spirit for the sake of food and happiness. But he was by no means a defender of the old bourgeois world; he was also a socialist on Orthodox grounds, a socialist with Christ. He constructed a theocratic Utopia which is a denial of the old world, a denial of the State and of bourgeois life. In this he was very Russian. Towards the end of his life Dostoyevsky turned bitter and joined the reactionaries, but they could not understand him. But both Tolstoi and Dostoyevsky rebelled against the injustices of human laws; they expressed the Russian spirit of antinomianism; they were both enemies of the bourgeois world and its standards. Both of them, though in different ways, seek true Christianity as against the distortions of historical Christianity, and Tolstoi and Dostoyevsky were possible only in a society which was moving towards revolution, in which explosive materials were accumulating. Dostoyevsky preached a spiritual communism, the responsibility of all for each: that was how he understood Russian *sobornost*;[1] his

[1] The inward, organic and harmonious aspect of Catholicity. See an article by G. Florovsky in *The Church of God*. S.P.C.K. 1934.

Christ could not be adapted to the standards of bourgeois civilization. Tolstoi did not know Christ; he knew only the teaching of Christ, but he preached the virtues of Christian communism; he rejected private property; he rejected all economic inequalities.

The thoughts of Dostoyevsky and Tolstoi are on the verge of eschatology, as is all revolutionary thought. Both Tolstoi and Dostoyevsky preach *fsyechelovechnost*, and that is a Russian idea. Internationalism is a distortion of the Russian idea of *fsyechelovechnost* and of Christian universality. According to Dostoyevsky the Russian people are the Christopher among the nations, they carry God into human life precisely because they have this all-human idea, the idea of an all-human brotherhood. Dostoyevsky was inconsistent in his attitude to the West, which he both loved and hated. There was an inconsistency too between the universal all-human idea which he ascribed to the Russian people and his sharp national antipathies. He believed that light would come from the East, but particularism and nationalism, which were always alien from original Russian thought, were no part of his mental outlook. On Russian soil nationalism was always a borrowing from the German. Tolstoi and Dostoyevsky were the mouthpieces of a universal revolution of the spirit; they would have been horrified at the Russian communist revolution with its denial of the spirit; and yet they were its forerunners.

Konstantine Leontyev is a figure of great interest and significance in this matter of foreboding and prediction in Russian literature.(22) K. Leontyev was an artist, a publicist and a sociologist. He was an entirely original thinker and belonged to no school or current of thought. He is usually considered a reactionary, but he was a romantic reactionary. He wanted to arrest the liberal equalitarian progress, because it led to the reign of pettiness and the ruin of complex and flourishing culture. To him socialism meant the reign of the bourgeois spirit, a grey earthly paradise, a levelling down and a loss of individuality. Like Hertzen the revolutionary, Leontyev the reactionary states acutely that characteristically Russian problem, the problem of the petty shop-keeper. A hatred of the bourgeois spirit was the determining factor of

Leontyev's life. He could not endure the thought that 'the Apostles preached, the martyrs suffered, poets sang, painters painted and knights glittered in the lists simply in order that the French or German or Russian bourgeois in his horrible and ludicrous clothes might live an individual and collective life complacently on the ruins of all the greatness of the past'.

Leontyev was a man of the sixteenth century Italian renaissance, but he became a monk; at first secretly, but later he lived in the Optima Pustina under the guidance of the Starets Ambrose. Aestheticism was a salient feature in his character; æsthetic values were to him fundamental. To the end of his life there remained in him an invincible two-sidedness; he was a monk in relation to the world to come—to heaven, and an æsthete in relation to this world—to earth; he did not desire the realization of Christianity in life, the realization of social justice, because that appeared to him to mean the death of beauty, it meant ugliness. Leontyev's Christianity was pessimistic and entirely other-worldly. In many respects Leontyev was a forerunner of Nietzsche. The will to power, an aristocratic approach to things, a tragic feeling for life, æstheticism, a-moralism, the concentration of attention upon the conditions in which cultures bloom and perish, all this links Leontyev with Nietzsche.

Leontyev's predictions about the Russian revolution are of particular interest for our subject. At one time he still believed that the flowering of an original non-bourgeois culture was possible in Russia, but later on he became disillusioned in the Russian people and the Russian mission; he went so far that he began to see the only mission of the Russian people in the fact that Antichrist will be born of them. Already in the 'eighties he feels that Russia is fatefully moving towards revolution and foretells what sort of revolution that will be. He foresaw the communist revolution in greater clearness and detail than Dostoyevsky. He foretold that the revolution would be tyrannical and bloody, that it would not be liberal but communist, that it would bring no proclamation of rights and of freedom and that the liberal radical intelligentsia would be overthrown. The revolution would not be humane and it would need the old instincts of domination and submission. Russian communism would attract the peoples of the East, and go on to annihilate the bourgeois world of the West. The destruction of the bourgeois world did not distress Leontyev in the least, but he desired to save the relics of noble aristocratic culture. For the sake of this, Leontyev was prepared to go to the length of proposing to the Russian Tsar that he should introduce communism from above. Leontyev, in accord with Russian tradition, hates capitalism and the bourgeoisie. Leontyev's forebodings and predictions are accompanied by a feeling of the coming of the end of the world.

An apocalyptic mood, and that with a pessimistic tinge, supervened in the Russia of the end of the nineteenth century. Behind this feeling of the coming of the end of the world and of the kingdom of Antichrist can be felt the impending end of a whole historical epoch, the destruction of the old world; and this feeling had two sides; it was sorrowful and it was joyful. Russian writers, the most interesting and subtle among them, had no wish to become reconciled to Russia's passing along the humdrum path of the West—bourgeois, rationalist, liberal, humanist. The apocalyptic mood takes an original form in Vladimir Solovëv, the most considerable of Russian philosophers. Solovëv's philosophy, like all original Russian philosophy, was Christian. To begin with, he constructed a Christian theocratic Utopia; he preached a free theocracy and believed in the possibility of Christian politics. In contrast to Leontyev he desired the realization of Christian righteousness in the fulness of life. He is a representative of Russian *fsyechelovechnost*, the foe of all national particularism; he is a Christian universalist; he thirsts for the union of the churches and at one time was inclined to Roman Catholicism. In the first period of his activity, Vladimir Solovëv interpreted Christianity optimistically; he desired to link it with progress and humanism; he believed in the possibility of the development of a divine humanity on the earth, but he lived through a series of disillusionments and suffered blow after blow; he was forced to confess that history certainly moves along no such path as that in which he saw the triumph of Christian truth. A keen sense of evil which before had been but weak now grew within him. At the end of his life he was finally disillusioned about the possibility of a universal free theocracy; he believed in the ways of history no more. He begins to think that history is coming to an end; it has no future· everything is exhausted; he writes his *Story of Antichrist* and in it he prophesies the speedy appearance of Antichrist. The world-wide organization of human society would not now be the work of Christianity, or of a Christian theocracy, but the work of Antichrist. Solovëv had a foreboding of the rôle of pan-mongolism and the danger threatening Russia and Europe from the yellow race, and—with Solovëv, as with Leontyev also—the apocalyptic mood, the sense of the impending end means not the impending end of the world, but the end of an historical epoch; it is a foreboding of catastrophes in history. This is an apocalypse within history. They all felt that Russia hung over an abyss.

N. Fedorov has an immense significance for the Russian apocalyptic mood. He lived at the end of the nineteenth century, but became known in the twentieth. With Fedorov the character of the apocalyptic mood changes. Of the religious philosophers he especially turns to the future and he understands apocalyptic actively, not passively. For a long while he was entirely unrecognized and unvalued, in spite of the fact that such great Russians as L. Tolstoi, Dostoyevsky and Solovëv valued him extraordinarily highly. In character, N. Fedorov was a Russian eccentric; he certainly was not a professional writer and philosopher. He was one of those Russians who looked for salvation from evil and suffering, who seek the Kingdom of God and have their plan of salvation. Fedorov considers that books should not be sold; they should be given away for nothing. This greatly hampered the spread of his ideas, but now, after the revolution, of all Russian religious thinkers of the nineteenth century Fedorov alone is popular, and in Soviet Russia there is a Fedorov school of thought. This is understandable. Fedorov considered himself an Orthodox Christian, but in him there were many traits allied with communism; he was a forerunner of modern actualism. Russian apocalyptic moods were of two sorts: there were revolutionary and there were reactionary sides to them. But without doubt the passive understanding of apocalyptic gained the ascendency. The Russian felt himself permeated by the mystical breezes of the impending end and foresaw the inevitable rule of Antichrist; he was in a condition of expectancy; the future aroused terror in him, that which the Apocalypse had foretold was coming to pass upon man; but man is not an active agent in the fulfilment of the prophecy. The apocalypse is understood as a divinely fated destiny; human freedom plays no part in it whatever.

With Fedorov the meaning of apocalypse undergoes a sharp change. Fedorov understood apocalyptic prophecy of the kingdom of Antichrist, the end of the world, of the Day of Judgment, conditionally, as a threat. There was nothing fated about it. If people would unite for the 'common task' of raising the dead for the true realization of Christian righteousness in life, if in brotherly union they would fight against the elemental irrational death-dealing powers of nature, then there would be no kingdom of Antichrist, no end of the world or Day of Judgment; then mankind would pass directly into eternal life. Everything depends on the activity of men. And N. Fedorov preaches an unheard-of activity of man, one that should conquer nature, organize cosmic life, overcome death and raise the dead. This 'common task' presupposes, as its indispensable condition, a brotherly attitude among men, bringing their differences to an end, realization of their kinship; but it is to be realized also with the help of science and technical skill. N. Fedorov believed that technical skill, if a united mankind wielded it in a brotherly spirit, could work miracles, even the raising of the dead. He understood philosophy in a practical sense. A class of learned and academic people, presenting pure knowledge abstracted from life, ought not to exist. The division between theoretical and practical reason is evil. Like Marx and Engels, N. Fedorov thinks that philosophy should not only take cognisance of the world but should change it. It should form plans for the salvation of the world from evil and suffering and especially from death as the source of all evil.

His posing of the problem of death of course distinguishes N. Fedorov radically from Marxism and communism. The life of the world is in the power of irrational elemental natural forces; these forces must be regulated and subjected to reason and knowledge. Man must secure the mastery over them. N. Fedorov appeals to people to cease fighting each other and to unite for the conflict against the elemental powers of nature. Here, no doubt, there is a likeness to communism, though resting on a different spiritual ground. N. Fedorov hates capitalism even more than the Marxists and considers it the creation of prodigal sons who have forgotten their dead fathers. He is also a collectivist, and the foe of individualism. His Christian faith and his recognition of a duty to the dead fathers distinguishes N. Fedorov from communism; but he is near to communism in his extreme activism, his belief in the almightiness of technical skill, his preaching of the collective common task, his hostility to capitalism, his practical thought, his totalitarian attitude to life, his inclination to control and plan on a world-wide scale, his repudiation of theoretical thought, speculation divorced from practical affairs, and in his recognition of labour as the basis of life. N. Fedorov was an original sort of communist; the basis of his thought was religious and there still remained in him unsubdued elements of Slavophilism. In his teaching realist elements were mingled with utopian; he was a typical Russian thinker. Among present day disciples of Fedorov the Christian elements in his teaching have become weaker and the technical elements, those akin to communism, stronger.

Russian literature and Russian thought bear witness to the fact that in imperial Russia a single integral culture did not exist, that there was a gulf between the cultured classes and the masses of the people, that the old régime had no moral support. Everyone had visions of bridging the gulf by some form or other of collectivism. Everything was moving towards revolution.

CHAPTER V

CLASSICAL MARXISM AND RUSSIAN MARXISM

I

Narodnik Socialism had spent its force by the 'eighties and the revolutionary movement could develop no further under its banner. The rise of the 'Popular Will' party, which set in the forefront of its objective the political purpose of overthrowing despotic monarchy by terrorism, had already meant the end of *narodnichestvo*. The revolutionary intelligentsia were disillusioned in the peasantry and resolved to rely solely upon their own personal heroism. The murder of Alexander II by members òf the 'Popular Will' party not only failed to bring about the triumph of the revolutionary intelligentsia but in the time of Alexander III led to a strong reactionary movement not only in the Government but also among the public. The revolutionary movement could find no social basis whatever.

At that time the group 'Freedom of Labour' came into being among the exiles abroad. At its head were G. Plekhanov, P. Axelrod, V. Zasulich, L. Deitch. This was the rise of Russian Marxism and the Social Democrat movement. After Marx and Engels, Plekhanov was one of the chief recognized exponents of Marxism. In past years Plekhanov had taken part in the popular revolutionary organizations, 'Land and Will' and 'The Black Redistribution'. After years of living in Western Europe, Plekhanov became entirely a Western and of a very rationalist sort, fairly cultured, though his culture was not of the highest kind; more of an armchair revolutionary than a practical one. He could be a leader of the Marxist school of thought, but he could not be a leader of a revolution; that was made clear at the time of the revolution.

But several generations of Russian Marxists were brought up on

[94]

Plekhanov's book—and among them Lenin and the leaders of Russian communism. Marxism on Russian soil was originally the extreme expression of Russian Westernism. The first generations of Russian Marxists waged war in the first place with the old tendencies of the revolutionary intelligentsia, with *narodnichestvo*, and dealt it irreparable injury. Russian Marxism looked for emancipation through the industrial development of Russia, which was the very thing that *narodnichestvo* had tried to avoid. Capitalist industry was to lead to the formation and development of the working class, which is the liberating class. The Marxists, therefore, were in favour of the proletariatization of the peasantry, which the *narodniks* had no desire to allow. The Marxists thought that they had found at last an adequate social basis for the revolutionary struggle for freedom. The proletariat in process of formation was the only social force which could be relied on. It was necessary to develop the revolutionary class-consciousness of this proletariat; it was necessary to go not to the peasantry which had rejected the revolutionary intelligentsia, but to the workmen in the factory. The Marxists considered themselves realists, because the development of capital was actually taking place in Russia at that time. The first Marxists wished to rely not so much on the revolutionary intelligentsia, on the part played by personality in history, as on the objective social-economic process. The Marxist assailed the utopian socialism of the *narodniks* with contempt.

If the typical Russian revolutionary of the *narodnik* party was predominantly emotional, the typical Russian Marxist revolutionary was predominantly intellectual. In accord with the conditions in which Russian Marxism arose, the Marxists from the beginning specially stressed the determinist and evolutionary elements in the teaching of Marx. They fought against utopianism and castle-building, and prided themselves on having at last found the truth of scientific socialism which promises certain victory, in virtue of the law-controlled, objective social process. Socialism will be the result of economic necessity, of an inevitable development. The first Russian Marxists were very fond of talking about the development of material productive forces as the chief ground of their hope and confidence. Thus they were interested in the actual economic development of Russia, not as a positive aim and a boon in itself, but because it supplied them with weapons for the revolutionary conflict. Such was their revolutionary psychology. The aims of the Russian revolutionary intelligentsia to all appearances remained the same, but they acquired a new weapon for the conflict; they felt the ground firmer under their feet. Marxism was a more complex intellectual theory than those upon which the revolutionary intelligentsia had hitherto relied, and required greater intellectual powers. But it was regarded as a revolutionary weapon, and above all as a weapon in the fight against the old tendencies which had shown themselves to be powerless. At first the Marxists gave the impression of being less extreme and violent revolutionaries than the old *narodnik* socialists or social revolutionaries as they now began to be called. The Marxists were opposed to terrorism.

But that was a deceptive appearance which led even the police astray. The rise of Russian Marxism was a serious crisis for the Russian intelligentsia—a severe shock to the foundations of their general outlook on life. From Marxism there sprang various new tendencies. And it is necessary to understand the nature of Marxism, its double nature, if one is to adjust one's mind to later Russian currents of thought. Marxism is a more complex phenomenon than is commonly supposed. It must not be forgotten that Marx was born of the German idealism of the beginning of the nineteenth century; he was permeated with the ideas of Fichte and Hegel. Like Feuerbach, who was the chief representative of left wing Hegelianism at the very time that he was calling himself a materialist, the whole man was saturated with idealistic philosophy and he even remained a theologian of a sort. Especially in the youthful Marx does one feel the idealist origin which has left its mark on the whole conception of Marxism.(23) Marxism, of course, gives very large grounds for expounding the Marxist doctrine as a system consequent upon sociological determinism. Economics determine all human life; upon it depends not only the whole structure of society but also all ideology, all spiritual culture, religion, philosophy, ethics, art. Economics is the basis, ideology the super-structure. There exists an inevitable general economic process by which everything is determined. The methods of production and exchange are the necessary starting points upon which everything else depends. In an individual human being it is not he himself who thinks and acts but the social class to which he belongs; he thinks and acts only as a nobleman, as a merchant—*petit bourgeois*, or member of the proletariat. A man cannot free himself from the economic position which makes him what he is; he only reflects it.

That is one side of Marxism. The strength of the economic factor in human life is not an invention of Marx, and he is not to blame for the fact that it has so great an influence upon ideology. Marx observed this in the capitalist society of Europe which sur-rounded him. But he reduced it to a theory and gave it a universal character. What he discovered in the capitalist society of his own time he regarded as the basis of all society. He discovered much in capitalist society and said much that was true about it. But his mistake lay in taking the particular for the general. The economic determinism of Marx bears an entirely special character; that is, the exposure of the illusions of consciousness. Feuerbach had already done this for religious consciousness. With Marx the method of this exposure of the illusions of consciousness is very reminiscent of the assertions of Freud. The ideology which is only the superstructure—religious beliefs, philosophic theory, moral values, creativeness in art—reflects reality in consciousness in only an illusory way. The reality is primarily an economic reality; that is, the collective fight of man against nature for the maintenance of life, in the same way as, according to Freud, it is primarily a sexual reality. Existence reflects reality, but existence is primarily material economic existence. Spirit is an epiphenomenon of this economic existence. Marxism does not derive all ideology and all spiritual culture from economics directly but indirectly through class psychology, i.e., there is a psychological link in the socio-logical determinism of Marx. Although the existence of class psychology and the distortion of all ideas and beliefs by class consciousness is an undoubted truth, yet psychology itself is

[97]

particularly weak in Marxism. Its psychology was rationalistic and completely out of date.

In order to understand the meaning of the sociological determinism of Marxism and of the illusions of consciousness which it exposes, one must turn one's attention to the existence of an entirely different side of Marxism, which is apparently a contradiction of economic materialism. Marxism is not only a doctrine of historical and economic materialism, concerned with the complete dependence of man on economics, it is also a doctrine of deliverance, of the messianic vocation of the proletariat, of the future perfect society in which man will not be dependent on economics, of the power and victory of man over the irrational forces of nature and society. There is the soul of Marxism, not in its economic determinism. In a capitalist society man is completely determined, and that refers to the past. The complete dependence of man upon economics can be explained as a sin of the past. But the future is otherwise; man can be freed from slavery. And the active agent which frees humanity from slavery and establishes the best life, is the proletariat. To it are ascribed messianic attributes, to it are transferred the attributes of the chosen people of God; it is the new Israel. This is a secularization of the ancient Hebrew messianic consciousness. The lever with which it will be possible to turn the world upside down has been found. And there Marx's materialism turns into extreme idealism.

Marx discovers in capitalism a process of dehumanization which makes man dependent upon the products of his own creation. To this is due Marx's brilliant doctrine about the fetishism of goods. Everything in history and in social life is the product of human activity, human labour, human conflict.(24) But man falls a victim to illusory, deceptive consciousness, as an effect of which the result of his own activity and labour presents itself to him as an objective world of things upon which he depends. The objective economic reality of things does not exist in itself—it is an illusion; only human activity exists and the active relation of man to man. Capital is not an objective material reality, existing outside man, capital is only the social relation of man with man in industry.

[98]

Behind the economic reality are always hidden living people and social groups of people. And man, by his own activity, can always dissipate this phantom world of capitalist economics. To this task the proletariat is called, and it falls a victim to this illusion of making the products of human toil into fetishes and independent entities. It is the duty of the proletariat to combat the dependence of man upon the products of human toil, to fight against the dehumanizing of economic life, to bring to light the almightiness of human activity.

This is an entirely different side of Marxism, and it was strong in Marx when he was young. The belief in human activity was a subject he inherited from German idealism. It is a belief in the spirit, and cannot be connected with materialism. In Marxism there is an element of genuine existential philosophy, which reveals the illusion and deceptiveness of objectivity, and by human activity overcomes the world of independent entities. It is only this side of Marxism which can inspire enthusiasm and call forth revolutionary energy. Economic determinism humiliates man, only faith in human activity raises him—faith in an activity which can accomplish a marvellous regeneration of society.

With this is also connected a revolutionary dynamic conception of dialectic. It must be said that dialectic materialism is an absurd combination of words. There cannot be a dialectic of matter; dialectic presupposes logos, meaning; dialectic of idea and spirit is alone possible. But Marx transferred the nature of thought and spirit to matter. It appears that the material process has its own thought, reason, freedom and creative activity, and, therefore, the material process can lead to the triumph of rational interpretation, to the victory of social reason over the whole of life. Dialectic here turns into the exaltation of the human will, of human activity. Everything is then determined not by the objective development of material productive forces, not by economics, but by the revolutionary struggle of the classes; that is, by the activity of man. Man can overcome the power of economics upon his life. There must be, in the words of Marx and Engels, a leap from the realm of necessity to the realm of freedom. History is sharply divided into two parts—the past, which was determined by economics when man was a slave, and the future, which will begin with the victory of the proletariat, and will be entirely determined by the activity of man, social man, when the realm of freedom will come into existence. The transition from necessity to freedom is understood in the spirit of Hegel. The revolutionary dialectic of Marx is not, however, the logical necessity of a self-revealing and self-developing idea, but the activity of revolutionary man, upon whom the past is not binding. Freedom is necessity absorbed into consciousness, but that absorption of necessity can work miracles, can completely regenerate life and establish something new and unprecedented. Transition to the realm of freedom is the victory over original sin, which Marx sees in the exploitation of man by man. The whole ethical *pathos* of Marxism is linked with the exposure of exploitation as the basis of human society, the exploitation of labour.

It is clear that Marx confuses the economic and ethical categories. The doctrine of added value, which is what brings to light the exploitation of workmen by capitalists, Marx considered a scientific economic doctrine. But in actual fact it is primarily an ethical doctrine. Exploitation is not an economic phenomenon but primarily a phenomenon of the moral order, a morally evil relation of man to man. There is an astounding contradiction between the scientific a-moralism of Marx, which cannot endure an ethical basis for socialism, and the extreme moralism of the Marxists in the appraisement of life in general. The whole doctrine of the class struggle bears an axiological character. The distinction between 'bourgeois' and 'proletariat' is a distinction between evil and good, unrighteousness and righteousness, between what is worthy of censure and what is worthy of approval. In the Marxist system there is a logically contradictory combination of materialist, scientific determinist and a-moral elements, with elements that are idealist, moral, religious, and myth-creating. Marx establishes a real myth about the proletariat. The mission of the proletariat is an article of faith. Marxism is not only a science and politics; it is also a faith, a religion. And upon this its strength is based.

At first the Russians accepted Marxism chiefly from an objective-scientific point of view. What struck them most was
Marx's teaching that socialism will be the inevitable outcome of
objective economic development, that it is determined by the
actual development of material productive forces. This was
accepted as bringing them hope. Russian revolutionaries lost the
sense of having no ground under their feet, of being suspended
over an abyss. They called themselves 'scientific' socialists—not
utopian dreamers. 'Scientific' socialism became an article of faith.
But the solid hope which scientific socialism gives for the realization of a longed-for purpose is linked with industrial development, with the organization of a class of industrial workers. An
exclusively agricultural and peasant country gives no such hope.
Therefore, the first step for Russian Marxists was to overthrow
the *narodnik* world view, and to prove that in Russia capitalism is
developing and must develop. The fight for this theory, that in
Russia capitalist industry was developing and consequently a body
of workers was growing, took the form of revolutionary conflict.
In the eyes of the Marxists, the social democrats became almost
reactionaries.

But Marxism was taken in different ways. For some the development of capitalist industry in Russia meant hope for the
triumph of socialism. A working class emerges. Everyone must
devote his strength to the development of class-consciousness in it.
Thus Plekhanov says: 'Behind capitalism is the whole dynamic of
our social life.' In saying this he was thinking not of actual industry
but of the workmen. For others, and especially for the legalist
Marxists, the development of capitalist industry acquired an
adequate significance of its own and the revolutionary, class aspect
of Marxism receded into a secondary place. Such was first and
foremost P. Struve, the representative of bourgeois Marxism.
These Russian social democrat Marxists, who later on were known
as mensheviks, cherished the theory that a socialist revolution was
only possible in a country where capitalist industry was already
developed. And, therefore, a socialist revolution would be possible

in Russia when she ceased to be mainly a peasant and agricultural land. This type of Marxist always set great store by the objective-scientific determinist side of Marxism, but kept also its subjective, revolutionary class side. The continual talk of the first Marxists about the necessity of the development of capitalism in Russia, and their readiness to welcome its development, led to this, that L. Tikhomirov who had formerly belonged to the 'People's Will' party and later went over to the reactionary camp, accused the Marxists of being obliged to start by being Knights of the Savings Bank. The Marxists considered the *narodniks* reactionaries who supported obsolete forms of economics. The *narodniks* regarded the Marxists as supporters of capitalism and bound to contribute to its development.

And in actual fact Russian Marxism, since it had arisen in a country still not industrialized and with no developed proletariat, was bound to be torn by a moral self-contradiction which weighed upon the conscience of many Russian socialists. How is it possible to desire the growth of capitalism, to welcome this growth, and at the same time to regard capitalism as an evil and a moral wrong against which every socialist is called to fight? This complicated question gives rise to moral conflict. The growth of capitalist industry in Russia presupposed the turning of the peasantry into a proletariat, depriving them of their means of production, i.e. reducing a considerable part of the nation to a condition of beggary.

This double-mindedness in assigning the values of capitalism and the bourgeoisie is to be seen in Marxism in its most classical form. Marx, in so far as he took his stand upon the evolutionary point of view and recognized the existence of various stages in history, to which different values are to be assigned, set a high value upon the mission of the bourgeoisie in the past and the rôle of capitalism in the development of the material strength of mankind. The whole conception of Marxism is very much dependent on the growth of capitalism and adjusts the messianic idea of the proletariat —which has nothing in common with science—to capitalist industry. Marxism believes that the factory, and the factory alone, will create the new man. The same problem faces Marxism in another form. Is the Marxist ideology the same reflection of economic reality as all other ideologies, or does it claim to reveal absolute truth independent of historical forms of economic interests? This is a very serious question for the philosophy of Marxism: is that philosophy pragmatism or absolute realism? This question, as we shall see, will be discussed in Soviet philosophy. But the first Russian Marxists were faced with a moral problem and a problem of cognition, and it set up a moral and logical conflict. We shall see that this moral conflict was decided only by Lenin and the bolsheviks. It is precisely the Marxist Lenin who will assert the possibility of establishing socialism in Russia independently of the development of capitalism and before a working class of any great size was organized.

Plekhanov declared himself against confusing the revolution which was to overthrow the absolute monarchy with the social revolution. He was opposed to a revolutionary socialist seizure of power, i.e. to the communist revolution in the course it actually took. The social revolution must be waited for. The liberation of the workers should be the work of the workers themselves, not of a revolutionary clique. This needs an increase in the number of workers, the development of their consciousness; it presupposes a greater development of industry. Plekhanov was fundamentally the enemy of Bakuninism, which he regarded as a mixture of Fourier and Stenka Razin. He was opposed to sedition and conspiracy, to Jacobinism and belief in committees. A dictatorship can achieve nothing unless the working class has been prepared for revolution. He stresses the reactionary character of the peasant Commune as a hindrance to economic development. One must rely upon the objective social process. Plekhanov did not accept the bolshevik revolution, because he was always opposed to the seizure of power for which neither strength nor consciousness had been prepared. What is needed above all is the revolutionizing of thought, not an elemental upheaval, and a revolutionizing of the thought of the working class itself, not of a partisan organized minority.

But with such an application of Marxist principles to Russia, there would be long to wait for the social revolution. The very possibility of direct socialist activity in Russia would be made a matter of doubt. The revolutionary will might be finally crushed by intellectual theory. Thus, the more revolutionary-minded Russian Marxists were obliged to interpret Marxism in some other way and to set up other theories of the Russian revolution, to work out other tactics. In this wing of Russian Marxism, the revolutionary will overcame the intellectual theories and the armchair interpretation of Marxism. There occurred unnoticed a combination of the traditions of revolutionary Marxism with those of the old revolutionary outlook which had no desire to tolerate a capitalist stage in the development of Russia, with Chernishevsky, Bakunin, Nechaev, Tkachev. This time it was not Fourier but Marx who was united with Stenka Razin. The Marxists who were bolsheviks stood much more clearly in the line of Russian tradition than those who were mensheviks. On the basis of the evolutionary determinist interpretation of Marxism it is impossible to justify a proletarian socialist revolution in a peasant country, industrially backward and with a feebly developed working class. With such an understanding of Marxism one must rely first of all on a bourgeois revolution, on the development of capitalism and then, when the time comes, bring about the socialist revolution. This was not very favourable to the stimulation of the revolutionary will.

In consequence of the transference of Marxist ideas to Russia, among the Russian social democrats a tendency to 'economism' sprang up, which handed over the political revolution to the liberal and radical bourgeoisie, but considered it necessary to organize a purely economic trade union movement among the workers. This was the right wing of social democracy, and it caused a reaction in its more revolutionary wing. The division became more marked within Russian Marxism, between the orthodox, more revolutionary wing and the critical, more reformatory wing. The difference between 'orthodox' and 'critical' Marxism was to a large extent relative and conditional, for 'critical' Marxism was in several respects truer to the scientific determinist side of Marxism than was 'orthodox' Marxism, which drew entirely original (in respect of Russia) conclusions from Marxism, conclusions which could scarcely be accepted by Marx and Engels.

Lukatch, whom we have already quoted, a Hungarian, and the most interesting and philosophically cultured of communist writers, who writes in German and displays great acuteness of mind, makes an original, and, in my opinion, a true judgment about revolution.(25) Revolution is certainly not determined by the radical nature of its objects nor even by the character of the means employed in the struggle. The essence of revolution is *totality*, entireness, in relation to every act of life. The revolutionary is one who in every act he performs relates it to the community as a whole, and subordinates it to the central and complete idea. For the revolutionary there are no *separate* spheres; he tolerates no division of life into parts, nor will he admit any autonomy of thought in relation to action or autonomy of action in relation to thought. The revolutionary has an integrated world-view in which theory and practice organically coalesce. Entirety in every-thing—that is the basic principle of the revolutionary attitude to life. Critical Marxism might have the same ultimate ideals as the Marxism which was revolutionary, and consider itself orthodox, but it recognized separate autonomous spheres in life; it did not affirm totalitarian entirety. One might, for instance, be a Marxist in the social sphere, but not a materialist; one might be even an idealist. One might criticize this or that side of the Marxist world-view. Marxism in that case ceased to be an entire totalitarian doctrine; it became a method of cognition in social matters and of carrying on the social conflict. This is the opposite of revolution-ary totalitarianism. Russian revolutionaries in the past, also, had always been totalitarian. To them revolution was a religion and a philosophy, not merely a conflict concerned with the social and political side of life. And Russian Marxism had to work itself out, to fit in with that revolutionary type and that revolutionary totalitarian instinct. That is the meaning of Lenin and bolshev-ism. Bolshevism also defined itself as the only orthodox, i.e.

[105]

totalitarian integral Marxism, which refused to tolerate the breaking up of the Marxist world-view into fragments and the adoption only of separate parts of it.

This 'orthodox' Marxism, which was in actual fact Marxism which had been changed by being given a Russian form, adopted primarily not the determinist, evolutionary scientific side of Marxism, but its messianic myth-creating religious side, which gave scope to the stimulation of the revolutionary will, and assigned a foremost place to the proletariat's revolutionary struggle as controlled by an organized minority, which was inspired by the conscious proletariat idea. This orthodox totalitarian Marxism always insisted on the preaching of materialist belief, but it contained strong idealist elements also. It showed how great was the authority of an idea over human life, if it is an integrated idea, and answers to the instincts of the masses. In bolshevist Marxism the proletariat ceased to be an empirical reality, for as an empirical reality the proletariat was a mere nothing; it was above all the idea of a proletariat that mattered, and those who became vehicles for the expression of this idea might be an insignificant minority. If this insignificant minority is entirely possessed by the gigantic idea of the proletariat, if its revolutionary will is stimulated, if it is well organized and disciplined, then it can work miracles; it can overpower the determinism which normally controls social life. And Lenin proved in practice that this is possible. He brought about the revolution in Marx's name, but not in Marx's way. The communist revolution was brought about in Russia in the name of totalitarian Marxism—Marxism as the religion of the proletariat, but it was a contradiction of everything that Marx had said about the development of human society. It was not revolutionary *narodnichestvo*, but orthodox totalitarian Marxism which succeeded in achieving the revolution, in which Russia skipped that stage of capitalist development which to the first Russian Marxists had appeared so unavoidable. And it was clear that this agreed with Russian tradition and the instincts of the people.

At that time the illusions of revolutionary *narodnichestvo* had already been outlived; the myth about the peasantry had collapsed. The people had not accepted a revolutionary intelligentsia. A new revolutionary myth was needed. And the myth about the people was changed into the myth about the proletariat. Marxism broke up the conception of the people as an integral organism; it analysed it into classes with opposed interests. But in the myth of the proletariat, the myth of the Russian people arose in a new form. There took place, as it were, an identification of the Russian people with the proletariat, and of Russian messianism with proletarian messianism. The Soviet Russia of workers and peasants came into being. In it the notion of the people as a peasantry was combined with the idea of it as a proletariat, and that in spite of everything that had been said by Marx, who regarded the peasantry as a petty-bourgeois, reactionary class. Orthodox totalitarian Marxism forbade any reference to the opposition between the interests of the proletariat and those of the peasantry. That was the rock on which Trotsky struck, desiring as he did to be true to classical Marxism. The peasantry was declared to be a revolutionary class, although the Soviet Government had constantly to fight it, sometimes very bitterly. Lenin turned anew to the old tradition of Russian revolutionary thought. He pronounced that the industrial backwardness of Russia, the rudimentary character of its capitalism, is a great asset for the social revolution.

There will be no need to deal with a strong, organized bourgeoisie. There Lenin was obliged to repeat what Tkachev had said, and by no means what Engels had said. Bolshevism is much more traditional than is commonly supposed. It agreed with the distinctive character of the Russian historical process. There had taken place a Russification and orientalizing of Marxism.

III

Marxism brought the Russian intelligentsia to a crisis and made it recognize its weakness. This was a change not only in world outlook but also a change in spiritual structure. Russian socialism became less emotional and sentimental, more intellectually grounded, and tougher. The first Russian Marxists were more

European, more Western folk, than the *narodniks*. The will to power awoke in them, the will to obtain power, and the ideology of power made its appearance. The motive of compassion grows weaker; it is not there that the power lies to fight for revolution. Its attitude towards the people as a proletariat is not so much compassion for its oppressed unhappy condition, as the conviction that it must conquer, that it is the coming power and the liberator of mankind. But with all these changes of spirit in the intelligentsia, the underlying foundation remained the same, i.e. the search for the kingdom of social truth and righteousness, capacity for sacrifice, an ascetic attitude towards culture, an integral, totalitarian attitude to life, conditioned by the one great purpose—the actual realization of socialism.

At first, Russian Marxism was a composite phenomenon; it contained a variety of elements. This was made clear in its later stages. If one section of Russian Marxists valued above all their integral totalitarian world outlook, defended their orthodoxy, and were distinguished by extreme intolerance, if for them Marxism and socialism were a religion; in another section a differentiation took place between the various fields of culture; the religious wholeness was broken up and there occurred a liberation of the oppressed life of the spirit and of spiritual creativeness. The rights of religion, philosophy, art, and the moral life as independent of social utilitarianism received recognition, i.e. the rights of the spirit, which were denied by Russian nihilism, revolutionary *narodnichestvo* and revolutionary Marxism. Since they ceased to see in Marxism and socialism a religion, an entire world outlook which provides an answer to all the questions of life, a place was found for religious enquiry and for spiritual creativeness. However strange it may be at first sight, yet it is actually Marxism —at first critical rather than orthodox Marxism—which has supplied us with an idealist, and later on a religious current of thought. To it belong S. Bulgakov, now a priest and professor of dogmatic theology; and also the present writer.(26) A crisis took place in the world view which was directed exclusively to the present earthly life, and another world was revealed, the world beyond. An end came to the exclusive reign of materialism and positivism among the Russian intelligentsia.

A fierce battle was fought in defence of the possibility of such a metaphysical and religious change of front. The idealist tendency was greeted with fearful hostility, alike in the Marxist and in the old *narodnik* and radical camps. This change of front looked like a betrayal of the fight for freedom. In the Marxist camp this originally took the form of a conflict between the orthodox, i.e. totalitarian tendency, and the critical, which permitted the union of Marxism with another, non-materialist philosophy, and a critical revision of certain sides of Marxism. In its later development this movement broke away from its connection with the various forms of Marxism and became a fight for the independence of spiritual values in cognition, in art and in the moral and religious life. Its adherents strove to give to socialism an ideological ethical basis. This was a triumph over the tradition of Russian nihilism, utopianism, materialism and positivism. In the last resort it came to this, that they began to look for entirety, totalitarianism, not in revolution but in religion.

At the beginning of the twentieth century there was a real cultural renaissance in Russia—religious, philosophical and æsthetic. And with it occurred a return to the traditions of the great Russian literature and Russian religious-philosophical thought. From Chernishevsky and Plekhanov they turned to Dostoyevsky, L. Tolstoi, Vladimir Solovëv. But these cultural and idealist tendencies began to lose their connection with the social revolutionary movement; more and more they lost the broad social standpoint. A cultured *élite* was formed, which had no influence on the wide circles of Russian society. This was a new schism—and the history of the Russian intelligentsia has been rich in schisms. In this lay the weakness of the idealist movement. And it had fateful results for the ideology of the Russian revolution and its conflict with the spirit.

Among the intellectual *élite* at the beginning of the century there was a real renaissance of Russian culture; a Russian school of philosophy made its appearance, with an original religious philosophy. Russian poetry again burst into bloom. After decades of decline in taste there was a quickening in æsthetic consciousness; interest awoke in questions of the spirit, as was the case among us at the beginning of the nineteenth century. There appeared in Russia, perhaps for the first time, people of a refined culture, even bordering on decadence. It was a time of symbolism, metaphysics, mysticism. People of the Russian cultural level were at the height of European culture. Nietzsche had an enormous influence at that period; and his influence met with Dostoyevsky's. On the side of German philosophy, such thinkers as Schelling and F. Baader again aroused the greatest interest. They passed through Ibsen and the French symbolists. But Russian symbolism did not remain in the æsthetic and artistic sphere; it rapidly passed over into the realm of religion and mysticism. Russian thinkers, like Khomyakov, V. Solovëv. K. Leontyev, N. Fedorov, V. Rozanov, who had become half-forgotten or as yet but little known and appreciated, were rediscovered and received recognition. Interest in the 'enlightened', nihilist, *narodnik*, stream of Russian thought was lost. That was the time when, on the watch tower of Vyacheslav Ivanov (that was what they called the sixth-floor flat opposite the Taurida Palace where the most exquisite of Russian symbolist poets lived), the most subtle conversations on æsthetic-mystical subjects used to take place every Wednesday.

At that time the revolution of 1905 was raging around them. Between the upper and lower levels of Russian culture there was almost nothing in common—there was a complete cleavage. They lived, as it were, on different planets. In general, the movement might be characterized as an original Russian romanticism, but in that section of it which was directed towards religion it was a transition to religious realism. There was nothing reactionary in the cultural renaissance of the beginning of the century; many of its active spirits even sympathized very definitely with revolution and socialism. But interest in social questions had slackened and those who were active in spiritual culture had no influence whatever on the social revolutionary ferment that was going on; they lived in a closed circle of the *élite*. At the same time stormy quarrels were taking place between the bolsheviks and the mensheviks, and the bolshevik party organization was beginning to grow. Plekhanov, the head of the menshevist faction of the social democrats, was a bookish theoretician of Marxism, but not a revolutionary leader. The real revolutionary leader was Lenin, the founder of the Russian and world communist movement.

The split among the Russian social democrats, between the bolsheviks and the mensheviks, began with the Congress of the Social Democratic Party which took place in London in 1903. At that Congress the bolsheviks received a quantitative 'majority', the mensheviks a 'minority' of votes. The word 'bolshevism' itself has had a very interesting fate. Originally the word was absolutely colourless, and meant those who sided with the majority at that Congress. But later it acquired a symbolic meaning. With the word 'bolshevism' was associated the idea.of strength; with 'menshevism', of comparative weakness. In the upheaval of the revolution of 1917 the insurgent masses were captivated by bolshevism as a power which gives 'more', while menshevism suggested itself as weaker—it gives 'less'.[1] In origin, a humble word of little import, bolshevism acquired the significance of a standard, or slogan. The very word itself sounded vigorous and expressive. But it was very characteristic of the split in Russian culture that both bolsheviks and mensheviks and all active workers in the revolutionary social movement were not at all inspired by the same ideas which held sway in the higher level of Russian culture. Russian philosophy was alien to them; problems of the spirit did not interest them; they remained materialists and positivists. The cultural level, not only of the bulk of the revolutionaries, but also of the leaders of the revolution, was not high, their thinking was elementary. They remained alien to that influence of the spirit which spread over Europe and Russia at the end of the nineteenth and beginning of the twentieth centuries. The themes of Dostoyevsky, L. Tolstoi, V. Solověv, Nietzsche, of German idealism, symbolism —in general, the themes of Christianity—remained alien to them. There was a higher intellectual culture among the elements

[1]'Bolshe' is the Russian for 'greater', and 'menshe' for 'less'.

grouped around 'The Liberation Union', an organization formed in the years 1903–4 and presenting a broad liberal-radical *bloc* in the struggle for political liberty against autocracy. In this *bloc* the broad groups of the left intelligentsia tried to unite with the liberal workers of town and country self-government. In it also the more moderate social democrats took part. But this 'Liberation Union', in which notable intellectual forces played their part, was unable to assume leadership of the revolutionary movement, because in Russia a movement could then be successful only under socialism, not liberalism, and inspired without fail by a totalitarian world view. The elementary nature and the crudity of the ideas of the 1905 revolution, in which the legacy of Russian nihilism made itself felt, repelled those who were working for the cultural renaissance and evoked a spiritual reaction.

At that time there took place a re-assessment of values in the world view of the Russian intelligentsia. This found expression in the symposium *Landmarks* which made a sensation in its day, in which the materialism, positivism, utilitarianism of the revolutionary intelligentsia, its indifference to the highest values of the life of the spirit, were subjected to sharp criticism. A conflict was waged in defence of spirit, but the conflict had no wide social influence. In accordance with the ancient tradition of the Russian intelligentsia, the struggle for the spirit was taken as reactionary, almost like a betrayal of the struggle for freedom. Such was the pre-revolutionary cultural atmosphere; while within the revolutionary movement itself there was evidence of weakness and of the unpreparedness of the social democrat mensheviks and socialist revolutionaries who carried on the *narodnik* tradition.

This was the period of the Imperial Duma and the beginnings of the Russian parliament, which was still rather limited in its rights; the period of the formation for the first time of a great liberal party known as the Kadets, under the leadership of P. Milyukov. In the upper levels of Russian life, it appeared as if liberalism was beginning to play a fairly important part, and with it even the Government had to reckon.

But the greatest paradox in Russian life and the Russian revolution lies in this, that liberal ideas, ideas of right as well as ideas of social reform, appeared, in Russia, to be utopian. Bolshevism on the other hand shewed itself to be much less utopian and much more realist, much more in accord with the whole complex situation in Russia in 1917, and much more faithful to certain primordial Russian traditions, to the Russian search for universal social justice, understood in a maximalizing sense, and to the Russian method of government and control by coercion. (27) This was predetermined by the whole course of Russian history, but also by the feebleness of creative spiritual power among us. Communism was the inevitable fate of Russia, the inward moment in the destiny of the Russian people.

CHAPTER VI

RUSSIAN COMMUNISM AND THE REVOLUTION (28)

I

The Russian revolution was universal in its principles as is every great revolution. It was brought about under the flag of internationalism, but for all that it was profoundly national and became more and more national in its results. The difficulty of forming a judgment about communism is due precisely to this twofold character that it has—it is both Russian and international. Only in Russia could a communist revolution take place. Russian communism must appear to Western people to be Asiatic, and a communist revolution of that sort would scarcely be possible in the countries of Western Europe. There, of course, everything would happen in a different way. The very internationalism of the Russian communist revolution is purely Russian and national. I am inclined to think that even the active share of the Jews in Russian communism is very characteristic of Russia and the Russian people. Russian messianism is akin to Jewish messianism.

Lenin himself is a typical Russian. In his characteristic, expressive face there was something Russo-Mongolian. In Lenin's character there were typical Russian traits, and those not specially of the intelligentsia but of the Russian people—simplicity, wholeness, boorishness, dislike of embellishment and rhetoric, thought of a practical kind, a disposition to nihilist cynicism on moral grounds. In several ways he recalled the Russian type which found expression in the genius of L. Tolstoi, although it did not overcome the complexity of Tolstoi's inner life. Lenin was made of one piece; he was a monolith. The part played by Lenin is a notable demonstration of the rôle of personality in historical events. Lenin could become a leader of revolution and realize those plans of his which had been worked out long before, because he was not a typical member of the Russian intelligentsia. In him characteristics of the Russian sectarian intelligentsia existed side by side with characteristics of the Russians who had made and shaped the Russian state. He united in himself traits of Chernishevsky, Nechaev, Tkachev, Zhelyabov, with traits of the Grand Princes of Moscow, of Peter the Great and Russian rulers of the despotic type. In this lies his originality. Lenin was both an out and out revolutionary and a statesman. He combined revolutionary ideas of the extremist type and a totalitarian revolutionary outlook with flexibility and opportunism in the means employed in the struggle and in political practice. It is only such people who are successful and victorious. He combined simpleness, directness and a nihilist asceticism, with astuteness, almost with cunning. In Lenin there was no trace of revolutionary bohemianism—a thing he could not bear; in this he was a contrast to people like Trotsky or Martov, the leader of the left wing of the mensheviks.

In his private life Lenin liked order and discipline; he was a good family man; he liked to sit at home and work and did not like endless arguments in cafés, to which the Russian radical intelligentsia were so much inclined. There was no anarchic element in him; he could not bear anarchism, of which he always exposed the reactionary character. He could not endure revolutionary romanticism and high-flown talk. As president of the Council of People's Commissars and the leader of Soviet Russia, he was continually exposing this sort of thing in communist circles; he fulminated against communist swagger and communist humbug. He set himself against 'childhood's malady of leftism' in the communist party. In the year 1918, when chaos and anarchy threatened Russia, Lenin made unheard of efforts in his speeches to discipline the Russian people and the communists themselves. He appealed to elementary things, to labour, to discipline, to a sense of responsibility, to knowledge and learning, to positive constructiveness, and not to destruction only; he inveighed against high-flown revolutionary talk and exposed anarchic propensities. He exorcized the abyss and he checked the chaotic collapse of Russia; he checked it by despotism and tyranny. In these ways he is like Peter. Lenin preached a cruel policy, but personally he was not a cruel man; he did not like it when people complained to him of the cruelty of the Cheka; he said that it was not his business, and that it was unavoidable in a revolution; but probably he himself could not have directed the Cheka. In private life there was a great deal of kindliness in him; he was fond of animals; he liked to joke and laugh; he took a touching care of his wife's mother and often gave her presents.

These traits in his character gave Malaparte an excuse for calling him a *petit bourgeois*, which was not quite true.(29) In his youth Lenin had had a great respect for Plekhanov and behaved to him almost with veneration, waiting for his first interview with Plekhanov with passionate enthusiasm.(30) Disillusionment in Plekhanov, in whom he saw the pettiness of self-love, ambition, and a haughty contempt for his comrades, meant for Lenin disillusionment in people in general. But the first shock which settled Lenin's attitude to the world and life was the execution of his brother who had been involved in terrorist activities. Lenin's father was a provincial civil servant who served long enough to attain the rank corresponding with the military rank of general and conferring hereditary membership of the nobility. When his brother was executed society in the neighbourhood turned their backs on Lenin's family, and this too meant disillusionment in people for the young Lenin; a cynically placid attitude to mankind grew in him. He did not believe in man, but he wanted to organize life in such a way that people might live more freely and that there should be no oppression of man by man.

In philosophy and art and spiritual culture, Lenin was a very old-fashioned person; he had the tastes and sympathies of the people of the 'sixties of last century; he combined revolution in the social sphere with reaction in the spiritual. Lenin insisted upon the original and distinctively national character of the Russian revolution. He always said that the Russian revolution would not be as the doctrinaires of Marxism pictured it. In this way he always introduced a corrective to Marxism; he propounded the theory and tactics of the Russian revolution, and he realized it in actual fact. He accused the mensheviks of following Marx in a pedantic way and of desiring the abstract transference of its principles to Russian soil. Lenin was not a theoretician of Marxism like Plekhanov, but a theoretician of revolution; everything he wrote was but a treatment of the theory and practice of revolution. He never elaborated a programme; he was interested in one thing only— the seizure of power, and the acquisition of strength to achieve that; and for this reason he triumphed. Lenin's whole general outlook on life was adapted to the technique of revolutionary conflict. He alone, long before the revolution, gave thought to what would happen when power had been seized, and how the power was to be organized.

Lenin was an imperialist and not an anarchist; his whole thought was imperialist, despotic. Hence his straightforwardness, his narrowness of outlook, his concentration upon one thing, the poverty and asceticism of his thought, the elementary nature of the slogans addressed to the will. Lenin's type of culture was not very high; there was much which was inaccessible to him and unknown to him. Every refinement of thought and of the life of the spirit repelled him. He read a great deal and studied much, but he had no breadth of knowledge or great intellectual culture. He acquired knowledge for a definite purpose, for conflict and action. He had no capacity for contemplation; he had a good knowledge of Marxism and a certain knowledge of economics. In philosophy he read simply for controversial purposes, in order to settle accounts with heresies and deviations from Marxism. In order to expose Makh and Avenarius by whom the Marxist bolsheviks, Bogdanov and Lunacharsky, were attracted, Lenin read a whole philosophical literature. But he had no philosophical culture, less than Plekhanov had; he fought all his life for that integral totalitarian view of life, which was necessary for the struggle and for the focusing of revolutionary energy. From this totalitarian system he would not suffer a single brick to be removed, he demanded the acceptance of all of it as a whole, and from his point of view he was right. He was right in thinking that the attraction of Avenarius and Makh or Nietzsche would make a breach in the wholeness of the bolshevik outlook and weaken it for the struggle. He fought for wholeness and consistency in the conflict. The latter was impossible without an integrated dogmatic outlook, without a dogmatic confession of faith, without orthodoxy. He demanded deliberate thought and discipline in the struggle against everything elemental; this was his basic theme.

He permitted any method in the fight to achieve revolution. To him 'good' was everything which served the revolution; 'evil' everything which hindered it. Lenin's revolutionary principles have a moral source; he could not endure injustice, oppression and exploitation, but he became so obsessed with the maximalist revolutionary idea, that in the end he lost the immediate sense of the difference between good and evil; he lost the direct relationship to living people; he permitted fraud, deceit, violence, cruelty. Lenin was not a vicious man; there was a great deal that was good in him; he was unmercenary, absolutely devoted to an idea; he was not even a particularly ambitious man or a great lover of power; he thought but little about himself; but the sole obsession of a single idea led to a dreadful narrowing of thought and to a moral transformation which permitted entirely immoral methods of carrying on the conflict. Lenin was a man of fate; therein lay his strength.

Lenin was a revolutionary to the marrow, precisely because through his whole life he defended an integral totalitarian outlook of life and permitted no infringement of it whatever. From this arose a thing which is difficult to understand at first glance—the passion, the fury, with which he fought against the smallest declension from what he saw as orthodox Marxism. He insisted upon orthodox views; that is to say, the views which agreed with the totalitarian general outlook about cognition, about matter, about dialectic and so on, from everyone who considered himself a Marxist and desired to be of service to the social revolution. If you were not a dialectic materialist, if in purely philosophical questions you favoured the views of Makh, then you were betraying the totalitarian integral theory of revolution and ought to be excluded.

When Lunacharsky attempted to talk about the search for God and the making of gods, although the discussion was of a purely atheistic character, Lenin attacked him furiously; and Lunacharsky belonged to the bolshevik group. Lunacharsky was introducing complications into the integrated Marxist outlook and that was enough for him to be excommunicated. Grant that the mensheviks had the same ultimate ideal as Lenin, grant that they also were devoted to the working classes, still they had not this integrated view; they were not totalitarian in their attitude to revolution; they complicated the affair by their talk of Russia needing a bourgeois revolution first, about socialism being realized only after a period of capitalist development, about the need to wait for the development of class consciousness among the workers, about the peasantry being a reactionary class, and so on. The mensheviks also attached no special importance to an integrated general outlook, to a compulsory profession of dialectic materialism; a number of them were ordinary positivists and even, what was really dreadful, Neo-Kantians, that is to say they held a bourgeois philosophy. All this weakened the revolutionary will. To Lenin, Marxism is above all the doctrine of the dictatorship of the proletariat. The mensheviks did not consider a dictatorship of the proletariat possible in an agricultural peasant country. The mensheviks wanted to be democrats; they wanted to rely upon a majority; Lenin was not a democrat; he asserted the principle not of majority, but of a selected minority; on that account they often flung the taunt of 'Blancism' at him. He drew up a plan of revolution and revolutionary seizure of power which by no means relied upon the development of consciousness among vast masses of workmen and upon the objective economic process. Dictatorship issued from Lenin's outlook as a whole. He even formed his general outlook to conform with the principle of dictatorship. He asserted dictatorship even in philosophy and demanded the dictatorship of dialectic materialism over thought.

Lenin's purpose, which he followed up with unusual logical consistency, was the formation of a strong party representing a well organized and iron disciplined minority and relying upon the strength of its integrated revolutionary Marxist outlook. The party had to have a doctrine in which nothing whatever is to be changed and it had to prepare for dictatorship over life as a complete whole. The very organization of the party, which was centralized in the extreme, was a dictatorship on a small scale. Every member of the party was subjected to this dictatorship of the centre. The bolshevik party which Lenin built up in the course of many years was to provide the pattern of the future organization of the whole of Russia, and in actual fact Russia was organized on the pattern of the bolshevik party organization. The whole of Russia, the whole Russian people, was subjected not only to the dictatorship of the communist party but also to the dictatorship of the communist dictator, in thought and in conscience. Lenin denied freedom within the party and this denial of freedom was transferred to the whole of Russia.

This is indeed the dictatorship of a general outlook for which Lenin had prepared. He was able to do this only because he combined in himself two traditions: the tradition of the Russian revolutionary intelligentsia in its most maximalist tendency, and the tradition of Russian Government in its most despotic aspect. The social democrat mensheviks and the socialist revolutionaries remained in the stream of the first tradition only, and that in a mitigated form. But combining in himself traditions which in the nineteenth century had been in mortal conflict, Lenin was able to fashion a scheme for the organization of a communist state and to realize it. However paradoxical it may sound, still Bolshevism is the third appearance of Russian autocratic imperialism; its first appearance being the Muscovite Tsardom and its second the Petrine Empire. Bolshevism stands for a strong centralized state. A union was achieved of the will to social justice and the will to political power, and the second will was the stronger. Bolshevism entered into Russian life as a power which was militarized in the highest degree, but the old Russian State also had always been militarized.

The problem of power was fundamental with Lenin and all his followers; it distinguished the bolsheviks from all other revolutionaries. They too created a police state, in its methods of government very like the old Russian State. But to organize government, to subject to it the labouring and peasant masses, could not be a matter of the use of armed force alone, or of sheer coercion. An integrated doctrine was needed, a consistent general outlook, and symbols which held the State together were required. In the Muscovite Tsardom and in the Empire the people were held together by a unity of religious faith; so also a new single faith had to be expressed for the masses in elementary symbols. Marxism in its Russian form was wholly suitable for this.

Of extraordinary interest in understanding the preparations for the dictatorship of the proletariat, which is the dictatorship of the communist party, is Lenin's book: *What is to be done?* It was already written in 1902 while there was as yet no split between the bolsheviks and the mensheviks, and it provides a shining example of revolutionary polemics. In it Lenin is chiefly concerned to combat what is known as 'economism' and the trust in elemental impulses in preparing for revolution. Economism was the denial of the integrated revolutionary outlook and of revolutionary action. To this trust in elemental impulses Lenin opposed the consciousness of a revolutionary minority which was called to take control of the general process. He demanded organization from above, not from below, that is to say, organization of the dictator, not the democratic, type. Lenin ridiculed those Marxists who were always waiting for the development of the elemental impulses of society. He asserted the dictatorship not of an empirical proletariat which was very weak in Russia, but of the idea of a proletariat with which an insignificant minority could be permeated. Lenin was always anti-evolutionist and, in fact, was an anti-democrat, and that had its effect upon the youthful communist philosophy. Being a materialist Lenin was certainly not a relativist, and he hated relativism and scepticism as products of the bourgeois spirit. Lenin was an absolutist; he believed in absolute truth. It is very difficult for materialism to construct a theory of knowledge which admits absolute truth, but that did not disturb Lenin at all. His astonishing *naïveté* in philosophy was due to his integrated revolutionary will;

absolute proof is asserted not by cognition, not by thought, but by an intense revolutionary will, and his desire was to select people of that intense revolutionary will. Totalitarian Marxism, dialectic Marxism, is, in his view, absolute truth. This absolute truth is a weapon to be used for revolution and the organization of dictatorship. But a teaching which gives a basis to a totalitarian doctrine and embraces the whole of life, not only politics and economics but also thought and consciousness and all creative culture, can be only a subject of faith.

The whole history of the Russian intelligentsia was a preparation for communism. Into communism there entered the well-known traits—thirst for social righteousness and equality, a recognition of the working classes as the highest type of humanity, aversion to capitalism and the bourgeoisie, the striving after an integrated outlook and an integrated relation to life, sectarian intolerance, a suspicious and hostile attitude to the cultured *élite*, an exclusive this-worldliness, a denial of spirit and of spiritual values, a well nigh religious devotion to materialism. All these had always belonged to the Russian radical intelligentsia. If the remnants of the old intelligentsia which remain and have not joined up with bolshevism, have not recognized their own proper characteristics in those against whom they have rebelled, that is a historical aberration, a loss of memory due to emotional reaction. The old revolutionary intelligentsia simply did not think about what it would be like when it acquired power. It was accustomed to accept itself as powerless and oppressed, and power and ability to oppress seemed to it to be the child of another wholly alien type, while all the while it was its own child. Here lies the paradox of the final stage in the development of the Russian intelligentsia, its transformation in a victorious revolution. Part of it was converted to communism and adapted its psychology to the new conditions. Another part of it did not accept the socialist revolution and forgot its own past.

The War had already produced a new spiritual type, a type inclined to transfer war-time methods to the ordering of life in general, prepared to put the theory of violence into practice, and with a love of power and a great respect for force. This is a world-wide phenomenon; it is seen equally in communism and in fascism. In Russia there appeared a new anthropological type, a new facial expression; people of this type have a different gait, different gestures from those of the members of the old intelligentsia. Just as in the 'sixties with the appearance of the nihilists, the milder type of idealists of the 'forties was replaced by a harsher type, so under the conditions of victorious revolution, itself the result of war-time conditions, the same process took place on a much bigger scale. Moreover, the old intelligentsia, linked by origin with the 'thinking realists' of the nihilist period, plays the same part as the idealists of the 'forties played in the 'sixties, and represents the milder type. As the result of its memory being enfeebled by emotion, it forgets that it is descended from Chernishevsky who despised Hertzen as a mild idealist of the 'forties. The communists ironically called the old revolutionary and radical intelligentsia 'bourgeois', as the nihilists and socialists of the 'sixties had called the intelligentsia of the 'forties 'nobility and gentry'. In the new communist type the impulse of power and authority has crowded out the old impulses of love of justice and sympathy. In this type there has been produced a harshness which passes into cruelty.

This new spiritual type was very favourable soil for Lenin's plans. It became the material out of which the communist party was organized, and became the dominant power in a vast country. The new spiritual type called to rule in revolution was recruited from the workmen and peasants. It went through military and party discipline. These new people, from the masses, were alien to the traditions of Russian culture; their fathers and grandfathers had been illiterate, devoid of culture of any sort and lived entirely by faith. These people had a *ressentiment* in regard to those of the old culture, which in the moment of triumph turned into revenge. A great deal is explained psychologically by this. In the past the masses had felt the injustice of a social order based upon oppression and the exploitation of the workers, but they had meekly and peacefully borne their painful lot. But the hour had come when it would no longer endure and the people's whole structure of soul changed. This was a typical process. Meekness and peacefulness may turn into fierceness and ferocity. Lenin could not realize his plan of revolution and seizure of power without a change in the soul of the people. This change was so great that the people who had lived by irrational beliefs and been submissive to an irrational fate suddenly went almost mad about the rationalization of the whole of life without exception. They believed in a machine instead of in God. The Russian people having emerged from the period of being rooted in the soil, and living under its mystic domination, entered upon a technical period in which it believed in the almighty power of the machine, and by the force of ancient instinct began to treat the machine like a totem. Such switchings over are possible in the soul of a people.

Lenin was a Marxist and believed in the exclusive mission of the proletariat. He believed that the world was approaching a period of proletarian revolutions, but he was a Russian and he made his revolution in Russia, a country of an entirely peculiar character. He had a very particular sensitiveness for the historical situation; he felt that his hour had come and that it had come thanks to the War which had brought about the dissolution of the old order. He had to bring about in a peasant country the first proletarian revolution in the world. He felt himself free from any of the stereotyped doctrines with which the Marxists mensheviks bored him; he proclaimed a workman and peasant revolution, a workman and peasant republic; he decided to make use of the peasantry for the proletarian revolution, and he succeeded in this, to the embarrassment of the Marxist doctrinaires.

Lenin began with an agrarian revolution, making use of many things which the socialist *narodniks* had previously asserted. The revolutionary elements of *narodnichestvo* and revolt entered into Leninism in a changed form. The socialist revolutionaries who represented the old traditions were seen to be superfluous and were shouldered aside. Lenin did everything better, more quickly and more thoroughly; he gave more. This led to the proclamation of a new revolutionary morale, corresponding with a new psychological type and with the new conditions. Things were seen to be quite other than they had been in the days of the old revolutionary intelligentsia; they were less humane and permitted every sort of cruelty. Lenin was an anti-humanist as he was an anti-democrat; in this he was a man of the new epoch, an epoch not only of communist but also of fascist revolution. Mussolini and Hitler are to imitate him. Stalin will represent the final type of dictator-leader. Leninism is not, of course, fascism, but Stalinism is already very near fascism.

In 1917, that is to say, fifteen years after the book *What is to be done?* Lenin wrote *Revolution and the State*, perhaps the most interesting of all his writings. In this book Lenin sketched out a plan for the organization of revolution and of political power, a plan designed to hold good over a long period. The remarkable thing is not that he sketched this plan but that he carried it out; he foresaw clearly how everything would go. In this book Lenin constructs the theory of the part to be played by the State in the transitional period from capitalism to communism, a period which may be more or less protracted. There was nothing of this in Marx himself, who had no concrete vision of how communism would be realized and what forms the dictatorship of the proletariat would take. We saw that to Lenin, Marxism is first and foremost the theory and practice of the dictatorship of the proletariat. From Marx it was possible to draw even anarchic deductions and the absolute repudiation of the State. Lenin rebelled decisively against these anarchic deductions, which were obviously unfavourable to the organization of revolutionary power and the dictatorship of the proletariat.

In the future, certainly the State ought to die out as an unnecessary thing, but in the transitional period the rôle of the State must even increase. The dictatorship of the proletariat, i.e. of the communist party, means stronger and more despotic political power than in bourgeois states. In accordance with the Marxist theory, the State was always the organization of class rule, the dictatorship of the ruling classes over the classes that were oppressed and exploited. The State will die out and finally be replaced by an organized society after the disappearance of classes. The State exists so long as classes exist. But the complete disappearance of class does not take place immediately after the victory of the revolutionary proletariat. Lenin certainly did not think that after the October revolution in Russia communist society would finally come into existence. There would still have to be a preparatory process and a bitter struggle. During this period of preparation, when society is not yet entirely class-free, the State, with a strong centralized authority, is necessary for the dictatorship of the proletariat over the bourgeois classes to crush them. Lenin says that the 'bourgeois' State must be destroyed by revolutionary violence and the newly formed proletarian State will die out to the degree that the class-free communist society is realized. In the past the proletariat had been subject to the domination of the bourgeoisie. In the transitional period of the proletarian State, controlled by a dictatorship, there must be a crushing of the bourgeoisie by the proletariat. In this period civil servants will obey the orders of workmen.

In his book, Lenin relies chiefly on Engels and continually quotes him. 'While the proletariat still needs the State, it needs it not in the interests of freedom but in order to crush its opponents,' Engels writes to Bebel in 1875. Here Engels is clearly seen as the forerunner of Lenin. According to Lenin democracy is certainly not needed by the proletariat and for the realization of communism. It is not the way to the proletarian revolution. Bourgeois democracy cannot evolve into communism. A bourgeois democratic government must be destroyed for communism to be realized, and democracy is unnecessary and harmful after the triumph of the proletarian revolution because it is opposed to dictatorship. Democratic liberties only hinder the realization of communism, and indeed Lenin did not believe in the real existence of democratic liberties. They only mask the interests of the bourgeoisie and its dominance. In bourgeois democracies also dictatorships exist, dictatorship of capital, of money. In all this there is incontestably some truth. With socialism all democracy will die out. The preliminary phases of communism cannot give freedom and equality. Lenin says this frankly. The dictatorship of the proletariat will mean cruel violence and inequality.

In spite of the doctrinaire understanding of Marxism, Lenin asserted the obvious primacy of politics over economics. The question of a strong government is to him fundamental. In spite of the doctrinaire Marxism of the mensheviks, Lenin saw in the political and economical backwardness of Russia something advantageous to the realization of the social revolution. In a country of autocratic monarchy, unaccustomed to civic rights and liberties, the dictatorship of the proletariat is more easily brought about than in Western democracies. This is incontestably true. The age-long instinct of submission must be used by the proletarian State. K. Leontyev foresaw this. In an industrially backward country with capitalism but little developed it will be easier to organize economic life in agreement with the communist plan. Lenin found himself in the tradition of Russian *narodnik* socialism. He asserted that revolution would take place in Russia in a distinctive way, not in the Western way, i.e. in actual fact not according to Marx, not according to the doctrinaire understanding of Marx.

How and why will the violence of coercion, the absence of all freedom which characterizes the transitional period leading to communism, the period of the dictatorship of the proletariat, be brought to an end? Lenin's answer is very simple, too simple. Regimentation, coercion, iron-dictatorship must be passed through first of all. The coercion will be exercised not only upon the remains of the old bourgeoisie but also upon the workman and peasant masses, the very proletariat which is the dictator. Later on, Lenin says, people will become accustomed to preserving the elementary conditions of social life and adapt themselves to the new circumstances, and then the use of force upon people will be abrogated. The State will die out. Dictatorship will come to an end.

Here we meet with a very interesting phenomenon. Lenin did not believe in man. He recognized in him no sort of inward principle; he did not believe in spirit and the freedom of the spirit, but he had a boundless faith in the social regimentation of man. He

[127]

believed that a compulsory social organization could create any sort of new man you like, for instance, a completely social man who would no longer need the use of force. Marx believed the same thing, that the new man could be manufactured in factories. This was Lenin's utopianism, but it was a utopianism which could be and was realized. One thing he did not foresee; he did not foresee that class oppression might take an entirely different form, quite unlike its capitalist form. The dictatorship of the proletariat, having increased the power of the State, is developing a colossal bureaucracy which spreads like a network over the whole country and brings everything into subjection to itself. This new Soviet bureaucracy is more powerful than that of the Tsarist régime. It is a new privileged class which can exploit the masses pitilessly. This is happening. An ordinary workman very often receives 75 roubles a month, but a Soviet civil servant, a specialist, gets 1,600 roubles a month, and this portentous inequality exists in a communist state. Soviet Russia is a country of state capitalism which is capable of exploitation no less than private capitalism. The transitional period may be drawn out indefinitely. Those who are in power in it acquire a taste for power and desire no changes, which are unavoidable for the final realization of communism. The will-to-power becomes satisfying in itself and men will fight for it as an end and not as a means.

All this was beyond Lenin's view. In this he was particularly utopian and very naïve. The Soviet state has become like any other despotic state. It uses the same methods of falsehood and violence. It is first and foremost a state of the military police kind. Its international politics are as like the diplomacy of bourgeois states as two peas. The communist revolution was distinctively Russian, but the miraculous birth of the new life did not take place. The old Adam has remained and continues to act, if in another form. The Russian revolution was achieved under the flag of Marxist-Leninism, not of *narodnik* socialism which had an old tradition behind it. But at the moment of revolution *narodnik* socialism lost in Russia its integrality and revolutionary energy; it was played out; its force was halved. It could play its part in the February (still bourgeois) revolution of the intelligentsia; but it cherished the principle of democracy more than the principle of socialism and it could play no part in the October revolution, i.e. the completely matured socialist revolution of the masses. Marxist-Leninism absorbed all the necessary elements of *narodnik* socialism, but rejected its greater humanity, its moral scrupulousness, as obstacles to the acquisition of power. It was nearer the moral standpoint of the old despotic government.

II

Any judgment on the Russian revolution presupposes a judgment on revolution in general, as an entirely special and, in the last resort, spiritual phenomenon in the destinies of peoples. Rationalist and moralist judgments on revolution are entirely fruitless and so are such judgments on war, which is very like revolution. Revolution is irrational; it is a sign of the dominance of irrational forces in history. The makers of revolution may consciously profess the most rational theories and make the revolution on those grounds, but revolutions are always a symptom of the growth of irrational forces, and this must be understood in a twofold sense. It means the old régime has become entirely irrational and no longer justifiable in any sense; and that the revolution itself comes into being through the unshackling of the irrational elements in the masses. The organizers of a revolution always desire to rationalize the irrational element in revolution, but all the same they are its instruments. Lenin was an extreme rationalist; he believed in the possibility of finally rationalizing social life, but still he was a man of destiny, a man of fate, i.e. of the irrational in history. Revolution is destiny and fate.

Three points of view are possible about revolution: (1) The revolutionary and counter-revolutionary, i.e. the point of view of people actively engaged in it; (2) the objective, historical and scientific, i.e. of people who regard it intelligently but take no part in it; and (3) the point of view of religious apocalypse and philosophy of history, i.e. of people who have taken the revolution into their inward experience, lived through the suffering of it and risen above its daily conflict. The revolutionaries and counter-revolutionaries understand the meaning of revolution less than anybody. Revolutionaries usually do not understand the meaning of revolution, for it is not covered by their rationalist ideal. But since they face the future, they may be instruments in the hands of the highest Tribunal of Judgment for making its meaning realized. Whereas counter-revolutionaries, as men who powerlessly and fruitlessly face the past, are those upon whom judgment is passed, impenitent, and, being in this condition, understand nothing. Objective historians can explain a great deal in the examination of origins, in disclosing secondary historical causes, but they do not set themselves to understand the meaning of revolution. They usually speak from a certain distance and say that the revolution was necessary, predetermined by the past, but the revelation of its meaning is not the affair of historical science; it is the business of the philosophy of history. But even the philosophy of history can approach the problem of the meaning of revolution only if it is based upon a religious foundation. As a matter of fact, the philosophy of history is always in a certain sense a theology of history, and always has a religious basis, consciously or unconsciously.

Now a religious philosophy of history inevitably takes an apocalyptic colour, and for such a religious, Christian philosophy of history the fact is revealed that the meaning of revolution is an inward apocalypse of history. Apocalypse is not only a revelation of the end of the world and of the last judgment. Apocalypse is also the revelation of the continual nearness of the end within history itself, within time which is still historical, of a judgment upon history within history itself, an exposure of its failure. In our sinful, evil world an uninterrupted progressive development is impossible. In it much evil, much poison is always accumulating. In it the process of dissolution is always going on. Too often it happens that no positive creative regenerative forces are to be found in the community, and then judgment upon that community cannot be escaped; then inevitable revolution is ordained in the heavens; then a rupture of time takes place. An interruption comes, and those forces triumph which appear irrational from a historical point of view, but which, if we regard them from above and not from below, indicate the judgment of Meaning upon the Meaningless, the action of Providence in the darkness. The reactionary G. de Maistre was not a pure reactionary; he recognized this meaning of revolution.(31)

Revolution has an ontological meaning. This meaning is pessimistic and not optimistic. The revelation of this meaning goes against those who think that society can exist indefinitely in a peaceful and quiet condition while terrible poisons are accumulating in it, when evil and injustice prevail in it, behind seemly idealizations of the past. It is difficult to understand those Christians who consider that revolution is not permissible because of its violence and bloodshed, and at the same time regard war as wholly permissible and morally justifiable. War produces still more violence and sheds still more blood. Revolution, with its use of force and its bloodshed, is a sin, but war is a sin also, often a greater sin than revolution. All history is to a remarkable degree a sin, bloodshed and violence, and it is difficult for the Christian conscience to accept history; this is a fundamental paradox of Christian thought. Christianity is historical; it is the revelation of God in history and not in nature; it recognizes a meaning in history; but at the same time, Christianity could never find room for itself in history; it always passes judgment upon the injustices of history; it does not allow optimistic views about history. For that reason history must come to an end, must be judged by God, because in history the justice of Christ is not made a fact.

Revolution is a small apocalypse of history, judgment within history. Revolution is like death; it is a passing through death which is the unavoidable consequence of sin. As the end of history as a whole will come in the passing of the world through death to arise into a new life, so also within history and within the individual life of man an end periodically comes, and death, for resurrection into a new life. This is what gives revolution its horror, its grimness, its pattern of death and blood. Revolution is a sin and the evidence of sin, as war is a sin and the evidence of sin. But

[131]

revolution is the fate of history, the inevitable destiny of historical existence. In revolution judgment is passed upon the evil forces which have brought about injustice, but the forces which judge, themselves create evil; in revolution good itself is realized by forces of evil, since forces of good were powerless to realize their good in history. And revolutions in Christian history have always been a judgment upon historical Christianity, upon Christians, upon their betrayal of the Christian covenant, upon their distortion of Christianity. For Christians especially, revolution has a meaning and they, above all, must understand it. It is a challenge to Christians and a reminder that they have not made justice a fact of experience. To accept history is to accept revolution also; to accept its meaning as a catastrophic interruption in the destinies of a sinful world. To deny any meaning to revolution must bring with it the rejection of history also. But revolution is horrible, grim; it is ugly and violent, as the birth of a child is ugly and violent, as the pains of the mother who bears it are ugly and violent, as the child who is born is ugly and subject to violence; such is the curse on a sinful world. And upon the Russian revolution, perhaps more than upon any other, shines the reflected light of the Apocalypse. Judgments passed upon it from the point of view of what is normal, of normal religion and morals, of the normal understanding of law and economics, are all of them ludicrous and pitiful. The malevolence of those who made the revolution cannot but repel, but it cannot be judged solely from the point of view of individual morality.

In the Russian revolution there were, incontestably, features which belong naturally to all revolutions, but it is also a unique distinctive revolution accomplished once for all. It was the offspring of the peculiar character of the Russian historical process and the uniqueness of the Russian intelligentsia. Never again will there be a revolution of that same kind. Communism in the West is a phenomenon of another sort. During the first years of the revolution a legend sprang up among the masses about bolshevism and communism. To popular thought bolshevism was a revolution of the Russian masses, an inundation of the elemental forces of Russian nature. But communism came of alien parentage; it is Western; it is not Russian, and it imposed upon the people's revolution the yoke of a despotic organization. To put it in scholarly language it rationalized the irrational. This legend is very characteristic, and witnesses to the feminine nature of the Russian people, which is always liable to be violated by an alien male principle. That was the way the people took Peter. In the Russian revolution, as indeed in every revolution, occurred the chaining and unchaining of chaotic forces. The popular masses raised by the revolution at first threw aside all restraint, and the transition to the rule of the masses threatened chaotic collapse. The popular masses were integrated, disciplined and organized in the elemental force of the revolution by the communist idea and by communist symbolism. In this respect communism rendered Russia an indisputable service. Russia was threatened by complete anarchy, and this was checked by the communist dictatorship, which found the slogans to which the people agreed to submit. The dissolution of Imperial Russia had begun long before. By the time of the revolution the old régime was completely effete, exhausted and played out. The War consummated the process. It cannot even be said that the February revolution overthrew the Russian monarchy. The monarchy in Russia fell of itself. No one defended it. It had no adherents. The religious beliefs of the people by which the monarchy had been upheld had begun to break up. Nihilism which embraced the intelligentsia in the 'sixties had begun to spread to the masses. The semi-intelligentsia which emerged from the masses were definitely atheist and materialist. Malevolence was a stronger force than large-heartedness. The Church had lost its position as the guide of national life. The subjection of the Church to the monarchic government, the loss of the corporate spirit, the low cultural level of the clergy, all this had a fatal significance. There was no organizing spiritual force. Christianity in Russia was living through a profound crisis.

A fateful figure for the destinies of Russia was Rasputin. He was a man of the people; he belonged apparently to the sect known as Flagellants and he undoubtedly possessed mystical powers. It was said of him that he had gifts which make a man a *Starets*[1] and a saint, but he turned them to evil use. In him the terrible darkness in Russian life was concentrated. The relations between the Tsar and Rasputin are of a much profounder character than is commonly supposed. The last Russian Tsar is a tragic figure. He paid heavily for the sins of the past, for the sins of his dynasty. He believed sincerely in the spiritual meaning of royal power, and it was painful to him to feel the break between Tsar and people, and his isolation as Tsar. He desired union with the people. The Tsar had no intercourse with them; he was separated from them by the wall of an almighty bureaucracy, and all the while he felt himself spiritually to be the people's Tsar. And then, for the first time, he met the people in the person of Rasputin. He was the first man belonging to the masses who was given immediate access to the court. The Tsar, and the Tsaritza especially, believed in Rasputin as in the people. He became a symbol of the people and of the people's religious life. The Tsar sought for religious support among the tragic events of his reign; he desired the support of the Church. He found none in the upper hierarchy because that itself was in slavish dependence upon him. Rasputin, however, appeared as popular Orthodoxy not in immediate dependence upon the Tsar and capable of being a support to him. And clinging to Rasputin as to popular Orthodoxy, the Tsar and the Tsaritza (who had immense influence with him) brought the Church into dependence upon Rasputin, the Flagellant, who nominated the bishops. This was a terrible degradation for the Church and it completely compromised the monarchy. Rasputin, a muzhik, morally corrupted by his contact with the court, finally aroused even the conservative court circles of Russian society against the monarchy.

During the War, before the February revolution of 1917, all classes of society except a small number of the highest bureaucrats and court officials were, if not opposed to the monarchy in prin-

---

[1] A monk distinguished by his great piety, long experience of the spiritual life, and gift for guiding other souls. Lay folk frequently resort to *Startsi* for spiritual counsel. *Starchestvo* (p. 15) is an abstract noun describing the system. See *The Way of a Pilgrim* (Philip Allan, 1931).

ciple, at least opposed to the monarch and especially to the Empress. That was the end of the dynasty. In the past the monarchy had played a part in Russian history which was often beneficial; it had rendered signal services, but the part had long been played out. The Russian monarchy, which had its roots in religion, was condemned from above, condemned by God and principally because of its violation of the Church and the religious life of the people, because of its anti-Christian ideas of Cæsaro-Papalism, because of its false linking of the Church with the monarchy, because of its hostility to enlightenment. It was a judgment upon the Church also on its historical side. We shall return to this in the final chapter.

III

The Russian revolution could be brought about only by beginning as an agrarian revolution, and relying upon the discontent of the peasants and their old hatred of the land-owning nobility and the civil servants. The memory of the horrors of serfdom, of the degradation of the human dignity of the peasants, had not faded out among them. The peasants were ready to avenge their grandfathers and great-grandfathers. The world of the ruling privileged classes, especially of the nobility, their culture, their manners, their outward appearance, even their speech, was completely alien to the people, to the peasantry, to whom it was like the world of another race, a world of foreigners. It was only an agrarian revolution, which is not merely a social and economic revolution, but above all a revolution of morals and life, that made a dictatorship of the proletariat possible in Russia, or rather, the idea of the dictatorship of the proletariat, since a dictatorship of the proletariat and, in general, the dictatorship of a class, is an impossibility. This dictatorship was exercised over the peasantry also, and treated them with brutal violence, as, for instance, in the compulsory collectivization, the establishment of the *Kolkhozes*. But this violent treatment of the peasantry was perpetrated by their own people, by those who were sprung from the masses, not by the gentry, not by the privileged blue blood. The peasant is no longer addressed as 'thou' or, if he is, then he can say 'thou' also in reply.

An agrarian revolution means the end of a civilization based upon the dominance of the nobility throughout life. The nobility had already long ceased to be the leading estate it had been in the first part of the nineteenth century, when from it sprang not only great Russian writers but also revolutionaries. After the liberation of the peasants the nobility were ruined and dislodged by the growing bourgeoisie. A large part of the land belonged to the peasants, but with the low level of agricultural skill and the lack of social organization the lot of the peasants was hard, and among them there was constant discontent and dreaming of a new order of things. If no longer in an economic sense, yet at least morally speaking, the gentry still ruled in life. The remains of feudalism lasted on until the revolution of 1917. The régime still continued on a class basis. The existence of enormous estates belonging to a small group of magnates psychologically and morally aroused in the peasantry indignation and protest, all the more because the Russian gentleman did not usually administer his estates in person. This is even more, much more, a psychological and moral question than a purely economic one. To the Russian peasants the theories of Roman law about property were always strange. The peasants considered that the land was God's; in other words, it belonged to no human being. The peasants always considered the acquisition of land by the gentry an injustice, as they did serfdom. The communal collective ownership of land was much more to the mind of the Russian people and especially to the Great Russians, thanks to the existence of the commune.

The peasants dreamed of a 'Black Redistribution', i.e. a redistribution of the land among the peasants. In earlier days they even believed that the Tsar would do this. A revolutionary *narodnik* organization of the 'seventies called itself the 'Black Redistribution', to correspond with these feelings of the peasantry. The Russian communist revolution actually brought about this 'Black Redistribution'. It took all the land away from the nobility and private owners. Like every great revolution it brought about a shift of social classes. It brought down the ruling controlling classes and raised the masses who had formerly been crushed and oppressed. It dug up the soil very deeply and brought about almost a geological revolution. The revolution unshackled the strength of the workmen and peasants for the making of history. This gave communism its dynamic strength. An enormous vital power which had been hitherto unsuspected was revealed in the Russian people. With it, in actual fact, took place a lowering of the level of culture, for a high culture is always created by qualitative selection and in the comparatively restricted circle of the *élite*. In the revolution the bolsheviks came into power in an ugly way, with an ugly expression of face, ugly gestures, and this is not only due to the fact that they did not belong to the stratum of society in which cultural forms and manners are produced and which tallied with the understanding of beauty, but also to the fact that they had more hatred, revenge, *ressentiment*, which are always ugly; they had as yet no style of any sort, no cultivation. There is always an ugly side to revolution, in which those who are over keen to be true to beauty cannot take too active a part. The bolshevik masses, as a matter of fact, did introduce a definite style of life, that which is bred of war, and a disintegrating war. This is one of the principal factors in the Russian communist revolution. Rhetoric and theatricality (of which there was so much in the French revolution) do not come natural to Russians. For this reason the Russian revolution was cruder, though this fact perhaps gave it an advantage.

The Russian communist revolution owed a very great deal to the War. Lenin, like Marx and Engels, attached immense significance to war as the most favourable moment for introducing an attempt at communist revolution. In this connection there is an astounding inconsistency among the communists, an inconsistency which may give the impression of hypocrisy and cynicism but which they themselves explain as a dialectic relation to reality. Who is more indignant than the communists with the imperialistic war, and who protested against it more vigorously? It was precisely the communists, though they were not then known as such,

and were simply the left wing of the social democratic internationalists, who desired to paralyse the War or at any rate gave the impression of wanting to do so. But at the same time in Russia it was
precisely the communists who more than anybody else benefited
from the War. War brought them their victory. The communists
or the socialist internationalists who had protested against the War
saw very clearly that a world war could be nothing but favourable
to themselves. I do not think that one can convict them of insincerity and falsehood. It was a dialectic insincerity or falsehood.
Marxism considers in general that good is realized through evil
and light through darkness. Such indeed is its attitude to capitalism
as the greatest evil and injustice and at the same time as a necessity
for the triumph of socialism. In the capitalist factories the mighty
humanity of the future is prepared. As a matter of fact it was certainly not the wish of the communists that the War should not
occur; only they wanted to get rooted into the minds of the
masses that the war between capitalist states is that direful evil
which will make rebellion against it possible and necessary. Communism desired and desires war, but only in order that war between nations may be turned into war between classes.

The whole fashion assumed by Russian and world communism
was due to the War. Had there been no war, then all the same
there would have been a Russian revolution in the end, but probably it would have come later and it would have been different.
The unsuccessful war created the most favourable conditions for
the victory of the bolsheviks. The Russians are by nature prone to
maximalism, and the maximalist character of the Russian revolution was very true to type. Contradictions and cleavages had reached
their maximum intensity in Russia, but it needed the atmosphere
of war to produce the type of victorious bolshevism among us,
the new type of the bolshevik conqueror. It was the War with its
experiences and methods which regenerated the type of Russian
intelligentsia. War methods were transferred to the internal life of
the country. A new type appeared, that of the militarized youth;
in contrast with the old members of the intelligentsia he is clean
shaven, alert, with a firm vigorous gait; he looks like a conqueror;

he makes no bones about the methods he uses; he is always ready for violence; he is possessed by the will-to-power; he forces his way to the front; he wants to be not only destructive but also constructive and an organizer. It was only with the help of such young men drawn from the peasants, the workmen and the semi-intelligentsia, that the communist revolution could be brought about; it could not be done with the dreamy compassionate person who belonged to the old intelligentsia, and who was always ready to suffer.

But it is very important to remember that the Russian communist revolution came to birth in misery and from misery, the misery of a disintegrating war; it was not born of a creative abundance of strength. Revolution, as a matter of fact, always presupposes misery, always presupposes an intensifying of the darkness of the past. There is nothing more appalling than a disintegrating war, a disintegrating army, and a colossal army numbered by the million at that. The disintegration of a war and of armies creates chaos and anarchy. Russia was faced by such chaos and anarchy. The old government had lost all moral authority; people had no faith in it, and during the War its authority sank still lower. People did not believe in the patriotism of the government and they suspected it of a secret sympathy with the Germans and a desire for a separate peace. The new liberal democratic government which came on the scene after the February revolution proclaimed abstract human principles; abstract principles of law and order in which there was no organizing force of any sort, no energy with which to inspire the masses. The Provisional Government relied upon the Constituent Assembly, to the idea of which it was devoted in a doctrinaire sort of way. In an atmosphere of disintegration, chaos and anarchy it wanted, from the noblest motives, to continue the War to a victorious end at the very time when the soldiers were ready to flee from the front and to turn the national war into a social war.

The position of the Provisional Government was so difficult and hopeless that it is hardly possible to judge it severely and condemn it. Kerensky was only a man of revolution in its first stage.

Moderate people of liberal and humanist principles can never flourish in the elemental sweep of revolution and especially of a revolution brought about by war. The principles of democracy are suitable to times of peace, and not always then, but never to a revolutionary epoch. In the time of revolution men of extreme principles, men who are disposed to dictatorship and capable of exercising it, are those who will triumph. Only dictatorship could put an end to the process of final dissolution and the triumph of chaos and anarchy. What was needed was to provide the insurgent masses with slogans in the strength of which those masses would consent to be organized and disciplined. Inspiring watchwords were needed. At that moment bolshevism, which had long been prepared by Lenin, showed itself to be the one power which on the one hand could put an end to the dissolution of the old and on the other hand could organize the new; only bolshevism could control the situation. It only corresponded to the instincts of the masses and their real attitude to things, and it, like a true demagogue, turned everything to its own use.

Bolshevism made use of everything for its own triumph. It made use of the weakness of the liberal democratic government, of the unsuitability of its watchwords to weld the insurgent masses together. It made use of the objective impossibility of carrying on the War any longer when the spirit of it was hopelessly lost by the unwillingness of the soldiers to go on fighting, and it proclaimed peace. It made use of the disorganization and discontent of the peasantry and divided all the land among the peasants, destroying what was left of feudalism and the dominance of the nobility. It made use of the Russian traditions of government by imposition, and instead of an unfamiliar democracy of which they had had no experience it proclaimed a dictatorship which was more like the old rule of the Tsar. It made use of the characteristics of the Russian spirit in all its incompatibility with a secularized bourgeois society. It made use of its religious instinct, its dogmatism and maximalism, its search after social justice and the kingdom of God upon earth, its capacity for sacrifice and the patient bearing of suffering, and also of its manifestations of coarseness and cruelty. It made use of Russian messianism, which still remained, though in an unconscious form, and of the Russian faith in Russia's own path of development. It made use of the historic cleavage between the masses and the cultured classes, of the popular mistrust of the intelligentsia, and it easily destroyed such of the intelligentsia as did not submit to it.

It absorbed also the sectarian spirit of the Russian intelligentsia and Russian *narodnichestvo* while transforming them in accordance with the requirements of a new epoch. It fitted in with the absence among the Russian people of the Roman view of property and the bourgeois virtues; it fitted in with Russian collectivism which had its roots in religion; it made use of the breakdown of patriarchal life among the people and the dissolution of the old religious beliefs. It also set about spreading the new revolution by methods of violence from above, as Peter had done in his time; it denied human freedom, which had been unknown to the masses before, and had been the privilege of the upper cultured classes of society, and for which the masses had certainly not been roused to fight. It proclaimed the necessity of the integral totalitarian outlook of a dominant creed, which corresponded with the habits, experience and requirements of the Russian people in faith and in the dominating principles of life. The Russian spirit is not prone to scepticism, and a sceptical liberalism suits it less than anything. The spirit of the people could very readily pass from one integrated faith to another integrated faith, from one orthodoxy to another orthodoxy which embraced the whole of life. Russia passed from the old Middle Ages to a new Middle Ages, avoiding the ways of the new history with its secularization, its differentiation of various fields of culture, with its liberalism, its individualism, its triumph of the bourgeoisie and of capitalism.

The old consecrated Russian empire fell and a new one was formed, also a consecrated empire, an inverted theocracy. Marxism, itself so un-Russian in origin and character, assumed a Russian style, an oriental style approaching Slavophilism. Even the old Slavophils' dream of transferring the capital from St. Petersburg to Moscow, to the Kremlin, was realized by the Red communists, and Russian communism proclaimed anew the old idea of the Slavophils and Dostoyevsky—*ex Oriente lux*. Light proceeds from Moscow, from the Kremlin, a light to lighten the bourgeois darkness of the West. At the same time communism creates a despotic and bureaucratic state, called into being to dominate the whole life of the people, not only in body but also in soul, in accord with the traditions of Ivan the Terrible and the rule of the Tsars. Marxism in its Russian form proclaims the dominance of politics over economics, the power of the Government to change the life of the country in any way it likes. In its grandiose schemes which were always on a world-wide scale, communism makes use of the Russian disposition for making plans and castle-building which had hitherto had no scope for realization or practical application. Lenin desired to overcome Russian sloth, the product of the life of the gentry and of serfdom, to conquer Oblomov and Rudin, the 'superfluous people', and in this positive task it seems he was successful.

A metamorphosis has taken place, i.e. an Americanization of the Russian people, the production of a new type of practical man with whom day-dreaming and castle-building passed into action and constructiveness, of a technician, a bureaucrat of a new type. But here also the special characteristics of the Russian spirit had their say. The faith of the people was given a new direction, the Russian peasants now reverence the machine as a totem. Technical undertakings are not the ordinary matter-of-fact customary affair that they are to Western people; they have been given a mystic character and linked on with plans for an almost cosmic revolution.

Russian communism from my point of view is a phenomenon which is entirely explicable, but explanation is not justification. The unheard of tyranny which the Soviet régime presents lies under moral condemnation, however much it may be explained; it is a shameful and infamous thing that the most completely organized institution created by this first experiment in communist revolution should be the G.P.U. (formerly the Cheka), that is to say, a government police organ incomparably more tyrannical than the gendarmerie of the old régime, which fastens its grip even upon ecclesiastical affairs. But the tyranny and cruelty of the Soviet Government have no necessary connection with the social economic system of communism; it is possible to conceive communism in economic life united with humanity and freedom. This would presuppose another spirit and a different ideology.

IV

The Russian communist state is at the present moment the only totalitarian state in the world based upon the dictatorship of a world view, on an orthodox doctrine which is binding upon the whole people. Communism in Russia has taken the form of an extreme *étatism* which holds in an iron grip the life of a huge country, and that unfortunately is in entire accord with the ancient tradition of Russian statecraft. The old Russian autocratic monarchy was rooted in the religious beliefs of the people; it recognized itself and justified itself as a theocracy, as a consecrated Tsardom. The new Russian State is also autocratic; it also is rooted in the beliefs of the people, in the new faith of the working class and peasant masses; it also recognizes and justifies itself as a consecrated state, as an inverted theocracy. The old Russian monarchy rested upon an orthodox world outlook and insisted upon agreement with it. The new Russian State rests upon a world outlook and with a still greater degree of coercion requires agreement with it. The consecrated kingdom is always a dictatorship of a world outlook, always requires orthodoxy, always suppresses heretics. Totalitarianism, the demand for wholeness of faith as the basis of the kingdom, fits in with the deep religious and social instincts of the people. The Soviet communist realm has in its spiritual structure a great likeness to the Muscovite Orthodox Tsardom. The same feeling of suffocation is in it. The nineteenth century in Russia was not an integrated whole; it was divided up; it was the century of free enquiry and revolution. The revolution created a totalitarian communist realm in which the free spirit was stifled, free enquiry disappeared. In it the experiment is being made of subjecting the whole people to a political catechism. Russian *étatism* always had Russian anarchism as its obverse. The communist revolution in its day made use of anarchist instincts, but it arrived at an extreme *étatism* which suppresses every manifestation of those instincts.

The Russian people have not realized their messianic idea of Moscow the Third Rome. The ecclesiastical schism of the seventeenth century revealed that the Muscovite Tsardom is not the Third Rome; still less, of course, was the Petersburg Empire a realization of the idea of the Third Rome. In it a final cleavage took place. The messianic idea of the Russian people assumed either an apocalyptic form or a revolutionary; and then there occurred an amazing event in the destiny of the Russian people. Instead of the Third Rome in Russia, the Third International was achieved, and many of the features of the Third Rome pass over to the Third International. The Third International is also a consecrated realm, and it also is founded on an orthodox faith. The fact that the Third International is not international but a Russian national idea is very poorly understood in the West. Here we have the transformation of Russian messianism. Western communists, when they join the Third International, play a humiliating part; they do not understand that in joining the Third International they are joining the Russian people and realizing its messianic vocation.

I have heard that at a French communist meeting a French communist asserted, 'Marx said that the workmen have no fatherland. This used to be true, but now it is no longer true; they have a fatherland, that is, Russia, Moscow, and the workers should defend their fatherland'. This is absolutely true and ought to be understood by everybody. Something has happened which Marx and the Western Marxists could not have foreseen, and that is a sort of identification of the two messianisms, the messianism of the Russian people and the messianism of the proletariat. The Russian working class and peasantry are a proletariat; and the proletariat of the whole world from France to China is becoming the Russian people—a unique people in the world; and the messianic consciousness of the working class and proletariat is bringing about an almost Slavophil attitude towards the West. The West

[144]

is always identified with the bourgeoisie and capitalism. The nationalization of Russian communism, to which all bear witness, has its source in the fact that communism has come into existence in only one country, in Russia, and the communist realm is surrounded by bourgeois capitalist states. A communist revolution in a single country inevitably leads to nationalism and a nationalist standpoint in political relations with other countries. For example, we see that the Soviet Government is at the present time much more interested in its connection with the French Government than in its connections with French communists. Only Trotsky has remained an internationalist and continues to assert that communism in a single country is not feasible and necessitates world revolution. For this reason he has been ejected. He was not wanted because he did not fit in with the constructive national period of the communist revolution. In Soviet Russia now they talk about the socialist fatherland and they want to defend it; they are ready to sacrifice their lives for it. But the socialist fatherland is still the same Russia, and in Russia perhaps popular patriotism is coming into being for the first time. This patriotism is a positive fact, but nationalism can take a negative form. The danger from Japan and Germany strengthens Russian patriotism. A defeat of Soviet Russia would be a defeat of communism, a defeat of the world idea which the Russian people proclaim.

The Five Year Plan which is so amazing to many Western people is a very simple and prosaic thing. Russia is a backward country industrially. It must in some way or other be industrialized. In the West this process takes place under the capitalist flag, and according to Marx this is what ought to take place, but in Russia industrialization must proceed under the communist flag. In a communist régime this is only possible when enthusiasm for industrialization has been created, when it has been turned from the prose of life into poetry, from a hard fact of labour into mysticism, when a 'myth' of the Five Year Plan has been created.

But all this is being brought about not only with the help of enthusiasm, poetry, mysticism and the creation of myth, but by terror and the G.P.U. The people have been brought into a condition of state serfdom. The communist régime in the transitional period is a régime of serfdom. In spite of Marx and the bourgeois political economists I think that commercial development is possible even under communism. Even under the old régime capitalist commerce was developed in Russia under government pressure. Inevitable economic laws are the invention of bourgeois political economy; such laws do not exist; Marxism demolished them, but not quite finally. For the industrialization of Russia under the communist régime a new motive behind labour was required, a new psychological outlook; it was necessary that the new collective man should make his appearance. Russian communism put enormous efforts into the creation of this new psychological outlook, this new man. It achieved a greater victory psychologically than economically. There appeared a new generation of young people who showed themselves capable of devoting themselves with enthusiasm to the success of the Five Year Plan, who face the problem of economic development not as a matter of personal interest but as social service.

It was easier to do this in Russia than in Western countries where bourgeois psychology and capitalist civilization had struck their roots deep. Even the Russian merchant of the old régime who made his pile by crooked dealings and became a millionaire was apt to think this a sin, would try to pray his sin away and in his better moments dreamed of a different life, e.g. of pilgrimage or monasticism; so that even that merchant was bad material out of which to form a bourgeoisie of the Western European type. It is even possible that the bourgeois spirit in Russia will actually make its appearance after the communist revolution. The Russian people never was bourgeois; it had no bourgeois prejudices, nor reverence for bourgeois virtues and criteria, but the danger of becoming bourgeois is very great in Soviet Russia. Into the young people's enthusiasm for the Soviet régime the Russian people's religious energy has entered. If this religious energy becomes exhausted, so will the enthusiasm, and self-interestedness will make its appearance, which is quite possible even in communism. But in any case the Five Year Plan is not realizing socialism; it is realizing state capitalism; it is not the interests of the workers, not the value of a man and of the worth of human labour, which are recognized as the supreme value, but the state itself and its economic power. Communism in the period of Stalin may be taken as a continuation of Peter the Great's work. The Soviet government is not only the government of the communist party which professes to realize social justice; it is also a state and has the objective nature of every state; it is interested in the preservation of the state and in its power, in its economic development without which the government may fall. Inherent in every government is the instinct of self-preservation, which may become its principal aim. Stalin is a ruler of the Eastern Asiatic type.

Stalinism, that is to say communism of the constructive period, is being imperceptibly transformed into a peculiar sort of Russian fascism. All the characteristics of fascism are inherent in it, a totalitarian state, state capitalism, nationalism, 'leaderism', and a militarized youth. Lenin did not reach dictatorship in the present-day sense of the word. Stalin is a leader–dictator in the contemporary fascist sense of the word. Objectively the process taking place is one of integration, the assembling of the Russian people under the standard of communism. From the intellectual and the moral point of view I react antipathetically to the Soviet Government; that government has stained itself with cruelty and inhumanity, it is steeped in blood; it holds the people in a deadly grip; but at the present moment it is the one power which provides some sort of defence for Russia against the dangers which threaten it. The sudden collapse of the Soviet Government without any organized force in existence capable of taking its place, not for a counter-revolution but for creative development of the social results of the revolution, would be a danger to Russia and would threaten it with anarchy. This must be said of the Soviet autocracy, as it could have been said of the autocratic monarchy. There is growing up in Russia not only a communist but a Soviet patriotism which is simply Russian patriotism. But the patriotism of a great people must be a faith in a great and world-wide mission of that people; otherwise it would be restricted to a provincial nationalism and lacking in world perspective. The mission of the Russian people is recognized to be the realization of social justice in human society, not only in Russia but in the whole world, and this fits in with Russian traditions. But it is a terrible thing that the attempt to realize social justice should be associated with violence, crime, cruelty and falsehood, horrible falsehood. The abominable staging in the Soviet law courts of stereotyped 'confessions' by the falsely accused alone is enough to inspire aversion for the whole system.

V

Such was the character of the Russian revolution. It happened in such peculiar circumstances that ideologically it could fit in only with a very much transformed Marxism, transformed, that is to say, in a direction opposed to determinism. Marxism was used to prove the impossibility of the proletarian socialist revolution in Russia. If in actual fact economics are the determining factor in the whole social process, then in an economically backward Russia we must still await the development of capitalist industry and we can count upon only a bourgeois, not a proletarian, revolution. That is the view of sociological determinism. But the Russian revolution took a line which bore witness to the fact that economics are not the determining factor in everything. And so there has appeared in Soviet Russia the new philosophy of Marxist Leninism. It continues to regard itself as a Marxist philosophy, but a Marxist philosophy of the period of proletarian revolution. Marx still lived in the heart of bourgeois capitalist society where in actual fact everything was determined by economics and freedom was not to be seen. But Marx and Engels taught that a leap would happen from the realm of necessity into the realm of freedom, and that then only real history would begin, in which man, social man of course, will not be controlled by economics but will himself control them.

For the Russian communists that time has come; that is the feeling they have; they see themselves in the realm of freedom; they are not in a capitalist world; they are in the elemental tide of proletarian revolution, a thing which was still unknown to Marx.

They are not controlled by economics; they do not depend upon the necessity of capitalist development; they themselves, by their revolutionary activity, control economics in any way they like. They feel they have the power to change, by revolutionary activity, not only Russia but also the whole world; and the young Soviet philosophy is attempting to give a new interpretation to dialectic materialism. Its basic category is that of self-originating movement; (32) the source of movement lies within, and not in a thrust from outside coming from environment, as mechanical materialism thinks. Real freedom is inherent in matter, and in it is the source of activity which changes environment. The characteristics of spirit, freedom, activity, reason, are transferred to matter, that is to say, a spiritualization of matter is taking place. It is continually repeated in Soviet philosophical and sociological literature that the principal thing is not 'productive forces', that is to say, economic development, but 'industrial relations', that is to say, class warfare and the revolutionary activity of the proletariat. This revolutionary activity is self-originating movement; it does not depend upon environment, upon economics; it re-makes environment and controls economics in its own way; they want to construct a philosophy of activism, and for that, materialism, both mechanical and economic, is most unfavourable. The philosophy of activism, promethean, titanic, is, of course, a philosophy of the spirit as it was with Fichte, and not a materialist philosophy; but it is not permitted in Soviet philosophy to speak of spirit. Materialism remains sacrosanct. Hence the characteristics of active spirit must be transferred to matter; and this is what they are trying to do and thereby doing violence to logic and philosophical terminology. Materialism is imperceptibly turning towards a peculiar sort of idealism and spiritualism. Already in Marx himself, especially in his youth, as we have said, the doctrine of the illusion inherent in the capitalist system, that man is dependent upon the products of his own creative activity, gave grounds for this attitude. Materialism cannot be dialectic. Dialectic cannot be inherent in matter which is formed by the jostling of atoms. Dialectic presupposes the existence of the Logos, of a Meaning which is revealed in dialectic development. Dialectic can be inherent only in thought and spirit, not in matter. Dialectic materialism is compelled to believe in a Logos of matter itself, in a Meaning revealed in the development of material productive forces, that is to say, in the rationality of irrational processes.

Soviet philosophy is a state orthodox philosophy; it detects and excommunicates heretics. This orthodoxy consists in the assertion of dialectic materialism as the general line in philosophy. Heresy is either the assertion of matter to the exclusion of dialectic or the assertion of dialectic to the exclusion of matter. The first is the heresy of mechanical materialism represented by Bukharin and several naturalists; the second heresy is represented by Deborin, who was inclined to idealism. It is necessary to assert a dialectic which is also a revolutionary actualist philosophy and which continues to assert materialism. Logically this is impossible, but psychologically it cannot be avoided. Orthodox dialectic materialism, which recognizes the possibility of self-originating movement, of freedom for the revolutionary proletariat, has been decreed by the Central Committee of the Communist party. Stalin who is devoid of any philosophical training and has less understanding of philosophy than the young Soviet philosophers, among whom there are knowledgeable people, pronounces an *ex cathedra* judgment upon what is the true philosophy. In the same way Hitler too will be recognized as a judge of philosophical truth. This is characteristic of the dictatorship of a world outlook and of the authoritarian régime which is fundamental to it.

Soviet philosophy is a philosophy of social titanism. The titan in it is not the individual but the social whole. For it even the laws of nature are not binding. The unchangeableness of these is regarded as an idea which belongs only to bourgeois science and philosophy. The Marxist philosophy of Plekhanov, Kautsky and the mensheviks is regarded as bourgeois and belonging to the 'enlightenment'. Soviet philosophy is in opposition to the enlightened materialism of the eighteenth century. For it everything is controlled not by enlightenment of thought, not by the light of reason, but by the exaltation of the will, the revolutionary titanic will. Philosophy should not only take cognizance of the world but it should re-make the world; it should create a new world. The segregation of theoretical ideas in a particular sphere, the creation of a caste of scholars and academicians, is an achievement of the bourgeois world. Theoretical reason should be united with practical reason, philosophical work should be combined with labour, with social construction, and should serve the ends of the latter. Soviet philosophy enters into the Five Year Plan. Truth, and absolute truth at that, is known only in action, in conflict, in labour. The titanic exaltation of revolutionary will presupposes the existence of a real world upon which the action is consummated, the action of changing it. This is a necessary realist presupposition which they confidently assert is a materialist presupposition. Consciousness is conditioned by existence and occurs in existence, but existence is conceived as material although matter is conceived in an almost spiritual way. Philosophical controversies, which in Soviet Russia are prolonged over years and are then printed, are problems debated not so much from the point of view of truth or error as from the point of view of orthodoxy or heresy, that is to say, they are theological rather than philosophical controversies.

The philosophy of titanism presupposes a change in the understanding of what freedom means. Marxist Leninism, or the dialectic materialism of the period of proletarian revolution, gives a new meaning to freedom, and, in fact, the communist meaning is very different from the usual meaning. On this account Russian communists are honestly shocked and indignant when they are told that there is no freedom in Soviet Russia. Here is an instance. A Soviet young man went to France for some months with the intention of then returning to Soviet Russia. Towards the end of his stay he was asked what impression France left upon him. He answered: 'There is no freedom in this country.' The astonished retort was, 'What do you mean? France is the land of freedom. Everybody is free to think what he likes and to do what he likes; it is with you that there is no freedom.' Then the young man expounded his idea of freedom. In France there was no freedom and the young man from the Soviet Union felt stifled in it because it was impossible to change life in France, to make a new life. The so-called freedom there was of the kind which leaves everything unchanged; every day was like its predecessor; you might turn out a government every week but that altered nothing; and so the young man who came from Russia was bored in France.

In Soviet communist Russia, on the other hand, there was real freedom because any day might change the life of Russia, and indeed the life of the whole world; it might re-make everything. One day was not just like another. Every young man felt himself a world-builder; the world had become plastic and out of it new forms might be modelled. It was this more than anything which acted on him like a charm. Everyone feels himself a partner in the common business, which has a world-wide significance. Life is absorbed not in the struggle for one's own personal existence but in the reconstruction of the world. So freedom is understood not as liberty of choice, not as liberty to turn to the right or to the left, but as the active changing of the world, as an act accomplished not by the individual but by the social man, after the choice has been made. Liberty of choice divides and weakens the energies. Real constructive freedom comes after the choice has been made and the man moves in the defined direction. Only that sort of freedom, freedom for the collective construction of life in the general direction of the communist party, is recognized in Soviet Russia; and it is precisely this freedom which is actual and revolutionary. French freedom is conservative; it hinders the social reconstruction of society and leads to everyone wanting to be left in peace and quiet.

Freedom, of course, must be understood also as creative energy, as the act which changes the world; but if freedom be understood exclusively in that way, and what takes place inwardly before that act, that realization of creative energy, is lost sight of, then the denial of freedom of conscience and freedom of thought is inevitable. And we can see that in the Russian communist realm freedom of conscience and thought is absolutely denied. There freedom applies exclusively to the collective not to the individual consciousness; the individual person has no freedom in relation to the social whole; he has no personal freedom and has no personal consciousness. For the individual person freedom is simply adaptability to the collective whole. But when the individual has adapted himself and merged himself in the collective whole he acquires enormous freedom in relation to all the rest of the world. Freedom of conscience, and above all of the religious conscience, presupposes that there is a spiritual principle in the individual which does not depend upon the community. This, of course, communism does not recognize. We shall see in the following chapter that, for communism, the kingdom of Cæsar and the Kingdom of God coincide and are identified, and so in communism based upon materialism the crushing of individual personality is inevitable. Revolutionary communist ethics are inevitably merciless to the living concrete man, to one's neighbour. The individual man is regarded merely as a brick necessary for the construction of communist society. He is but a means to an end.

The interpretation by communism of the life of each man as the service of a supra-personal purpose, the service not of himself but of the great whole, is healthy, true and wholly in agreement with Christianity, but this true idea is distorted by the denial of the independent worth and value of each human person and of his spiritual freedom. There exists also in communism the true idea that man is called in unity with his fellow men to control and organize social and cosmic life, but in Russian communism this idea, to which radical expression was given by the Christian thinker, N. Fedorov,(33) took an almost maniacal form and turned man into a tool and a mere means for that control.

All these distortions are due not so much to the social and economic system of communism as to its false spirit. Freedom of the spirit is not denied by economics, which are powerless in relation to the spirit, but by spirit itself; by a spirit which is hostile to freedom. The militant anti-spiritual materialism of communism is a phenomenon of spirit, not of matter. It is a false orientation of spirit. Communist economics in themselves may be neutral. It is communist religion, not economics, which is the foe of Christianity, of the spirit, and of freedom. Truth and error are so intermingled in communism because communism is not only a social phenomenon but a spiritual phenomenon too. In the idea of a classless labouring society in which each works for others and for all, for the supra-personal purpose, the denial of God and of freedom need not be included. On the contrary, this idea is more compatible with Christianity than the idea upon which the bourgeois capitalist society is based. But the combination of this idea with a false world outlook which repudiates spirit and freedom leads to fatal results. It is the very religious character of communism, the very religion of communism, which makes it anti-religious and anti-Christian. A communist society and state profess to be totalitarian, but only the Kingdom of God can be totalitarian; the kingdom of Cæsar is always partial. For communism, Cæsar's kingdom becomes God's—exactly as in German national socialism, only more consistently and radically. And this too inevitably evokes spiritual conflict.

It is a fatal mistake to give this spiritual conflict the character of a social conflict, which is out to defend the old capitalist bourgeois society or the old régime. It robs the struggle against communism of all its strength. The whole world is moving towards the dissolution of the old capitalist societies, to the conquest of that spirit which has been their inspiration. The movement towards socialism, that is to say, socialism understood in a broad and not in a doctrinaire sense, is a world-wide phenomenon. This world crisis leading to a new form of society, the character of which is not yet clear, is being achieved by transitional stages. Such a transitional stage is what is known as 'linked' controlled state capitalism. This is a difficult process and it is accompanied by the process of making the State absolute. In Soviet Russia this stage, which is not yet socialism, finds much support in the ancient traditions of an absolute state. And there is much that is elementary in what is happening in Soviet Russia, the elementary civilizing of the working class and peasant masses as they emerge from a state of illiteracy. There is nothing specifically communist in this, but the civilizing process is accomplished by replacing the religious Christian symbols by the Marxist communist symbols. What is abnormal and unwholesome is that the associating of the masses with civilization takes place with the complete destruction of the old Russian intelligentsia. The revolution of which the intelligentsia always dreamed has come to be the end of the intelligentsia. This is owing to the age-long cleavage in Russian history between the intelligentsia and the masses, and also to the dishonest demagogy by which the Russian communists reached their triumph. It led to a terrible shortage of cultured man power. The idea of proletarian culture is self-contradictory and false from the point of view of communist ideals, seeing that communism seeks to destroy the existence of the proletariat as a class and must strive after culture for the whole community. This was understood by Trotsky.(34)

Russian communism, if one looks more deeply into it in the light of Russia's historical destiny, is a deformation of Russian ideas, of Russian messianism and universalism, of the Russian search for the kingdom of truth and righteousness, that Russian idea which in the atmosphere of war and dissolution assumed such ugly forms. But Russian communism had more links with Russian traditions than is generally supposed, not only with its good traditions, but also with some very bad ones.

For twenty-five years the celebrated procurator of the Holy Synod, K. P. Pobedonostzev, ruled the Russian Church and in ideas the Russian State also. He was the spiritual leader of the old monarchist Russia during the period of its decline. Lenin was the spiritual leader of the new communist Russia. He was for many years the dominant force in the preparatory process for revolution, and after the revolution he ruled Russia. Pobedonostzev and Lenin represented ideas which are polar opposites, but in spiritual structure there is a likeness between them. To a large extent they belong to one and the same type. Pobedonostzev was a more remarkable, complex and interesting person than one thinks when considering simply his reactionary politics. I once characterized Pobedonostzev's world outlook as 'nihilism on a religious basis'. He was a nihilist in relation to man and the world; he had absolutely no belief in man; he considered human nature absolutely bad and contemptible. A contemptuous and disparaging attitude to human life and to the life of the world grew upon him, and this attitude of his extended to the bishops with whom he came into contact as procurator of the Holy Synod. He despised the bishops and refused to see any sort of human spiritual qualities in them, and considered that the representative of the State should control the bishops. As procurator of the Holy Synod he subordinated the Church to the State because he did not believe in the human qualities of either bishops or lay folk. Man was so hopelessly bad that his only salvation lay in being ruled with a rod of iron. You must not give freedom to man. Only by the violence and coercion of monarchist government could the world be held in check.

From his disbelief in man and his nihilist attitude to the world, Pobedonostzev drew most extreme reactionary conclusions. He believed in God, but he could not transfer this belief in God to his relations with men and the world. In his private life this man, who acquired the reputation of a grand inquisitor, was gentle; he was touchingly fond of children; he was afraid of his wife and was not in the least ferocious to his 'neighbour'. He had no love for 'the man far off', for man, humanity, progress, freedom, equality and so on. Can there be any likeness then between him and Lenin? Lenin also had no belief in man, and he also adopted a nihilist attitude to the world; he had a cynical contempt for man and he too saw salvation only in ruling man with a rod of iron. Like Pobedonostzev he thought that it was only possible to organize human life by coercion and force. As Pobedonostzev despised the ecclesiastical hierarchy over whom he had control, so also Lenin despised the revolutionary hierarchy which he controlled. He referred to the communists in mocking language and had no belief in their human qualities. Both men alike believed in regimentation, in the forcible organization of the people, as the only way out. Society cannot be based upon human qualities. It must be so organized that the hopelessly bad human material shall be subjected to regimentation and made accustomed to the conditions of life lived as a community.

Lenin also taught that the world and man are ruined by sin, and to him the sin was the exploitation of man by man, the sin of class inequality. Lenin did not believe in human nature, in the highest principle in man, but he did not believe in God, as Pobedonostzev believed. He believed in a future life, not in the world to come but in a future life in this world, in the new communist society which for him took the place of God. He believed in the victory of the proletariat which to him was the New Israel. But the communist society is to be realized not in the strength of people's good qualities but by the power of regimentation, compulsion, organization. Lenin's communist government is just as authoritative and autocratic as the monarchist government of Pobedonostzev. From his disbelief in man and from his nihilist attitude to the life of the world, Lenin drew the reverse conclusion, an extreme revolutionary conclusion. An extreme revolutionary and an extreme reactionary conclusion can both alike be drawn, but the life of this world was vain and evil both for Lenin and for Pobedonostzev. Like Pobedonostzev, Lenin too in his private life was not an evil man; there was no little kindliness in him and a human attitude to his neighbour. Lenin also loved children and animals; he was not an inquisitor. It is an astounding thing in the destiny of Russia and the Russian people that up to the revolution Russia was ruled by a man who did not believe in man and took a nihilist attitude to the world, and after the revolution by a man who also did not believe in man and took a nihilist attitude to the world. This is highly symbolic and explains a great deal. A Russian government cannot become humane, and the obverse of this fact is Russian anarchism. A nihilist attitude to the world and to man is a distorted form of ascetic Orthodoxy, and we now come close up to the last problem, the religious problem, to the relation between communism and Orthodoxy.

CHAPTER VII
COMMUNISM AND CHRISTIANITY

I

The question of the relation of communism to religion and particularly to the Christian religion requires special consideration. The implacably hostile attitude of communism to all religion is no accidental phenomenon; it belongs to the very essence of the communist general outlook on life. The communist state, in fact, is the dictatorship of a general outlook on life. The communist régime is extreme *étatism*. In it the state is totalitarian, absolute, and demands an enforced unity of thought. Communism carries on a persecution of every church, and above all of the Orthodox Church, on account of the part that it has played in history. Communists profess a militant atheism and they are compelled to carry on anti-religious propaganda. Communism in actual fact is the foe of every form of religion and especially of Christianity, not as a social system, but as itself a religion. It wants to be a religion itself, to take the place of Christianity. It professes to answer the religious questions of the human soul and to give a meaning to life. Communism is integrated; it embraces the whole of life; its relations are with no special section of it. On this account its conflict with other religious faiths is inevitable. Intolerance and fanaticism always have a religious origin. No scientific, purely intellectual theory can be so intolerant and fanatical, and communism is exclusive as a religious faith is.

The Russian religious temperament, Russian sectarian and schismatic psychology play an immense part here. But an implacable militant attitude to religion was fore-ordained by Marx himself. Marx in his *Introduction to the Criticism of Hegel's Philosophy of Life* said that religion was the opium of the people: a phrase which has acquired so definite a meaning in present-day Russia. Marx thought that for the liberation of the working class, and consequently of all mankind, it is necessary to tear religious feeling out of the human heart. Marx said, 'Not religious freedom of conscience but the freedom of conscience from religious superstition.' Religious beliefs reflect human slavery, slavery to the elemental powers of nature and the irrational forces of society. They exist only until man, social man, finally overcomes the elemental and irrational forces which surround him with mystery. In his thoughts on religion, Marx was the pupil of Feuerbach, but he developed Feuerbach's thoughts in a social direction. Feuerbach was the greatest genius in the atheistic philosophy of the nineteenth century, with a very acute mind and with many gifts for anthropological philosophy in general. Feuerbach, as is well known, desired to convert theology into anthropology; to him man was not made in the image and likeness of God, but God is made in the image and likeness of man. Religion is but the expression of man's highest nature, withdrawn from man, become alienated from him and transferred to the transcendental region of another world. Religion has impoverished and despoiled man; the poor man has a rich God. All his wealth is transferred to God and communicated to Him. Belief in God is the expression of man's weakness, poverty and slavery. The man who was strong, rich and free would have no need of God. Everything that was highest he would have in himself.

From this Marx drew the conclusion that belief in God keeps the proletariat in slavery, poverty and degradation. Religious beliefs give an illusory, fictitious consolation; they transfer victory into an unreal sphere and, therefore, are a hindrance to real victory and liberation. The triumphant proletariat will dispose of all illusory, fictitious consolations, consolations of the other world; it will realize victory here upon earth. Marx's teaching about the illusions of consciousness, religious and ideological illusions which reflect man's slavery and dependence, his weakness and humiliation, is taken from Feuerbach. But Marx gave the teaching about the illusory nature of consciousness a more sharply social character. Marx's militant atheism requires above all a change of

[159]

consciousness. Religious beliefs must be destroyed not by imprisonment and persecution but by revolutionizing thought; and this is to happen as a result of the revolutionary class war of the proletariat. Marx was particularly interested in the conflict against religious belief during his youth. To him it was above all an intellectual conflict, as it was also for Bruno Bauer. He found himself in the current of left Hegelianism. Later on his interest in questions connected with the working out of a general outlook weakened, and he concerned himself chiefly with economic problems, but he remained a militant atheist. Still it should be said that anti-religion with Marx took a less extreme form of expression than with Bakunin in Russia or with Düring in Germany. Düring, who represented a type of socialism opposed to Marxism, with an anarchist tendency, says outright that in socialist society religion will be *prohibited*. Engels who wrote his principal book in the form of a criticism of Düring's philosophical and social views, even takes exception to this prohibition of religion of his. Militant enlightenment usually assumes the form of militant atheism. Reason having mastered itself and liberated itself from the traditions in which it was shackled, set itself to oppose belief in God. This is always only a transitional stage in which reason fails to recognize how much it depends upon negative emotional reaction; and a more mature and actually more free reason recognizes its limits and changes its attitude to religious faith. Enlightening reason in Russia is in the first militant stage, and it is wholly swayed by the emotions. This is to be seen in Lenin.

Lenin was a passionate and convinced atheist and hater of religion. I use the word 'atheist', although I do not believe in the existence of pure atheists. Man is a religious animal and when he denies the true and living God he makes himself false gods, images and idols, and worships them. Lenin had very much coarsened Marxist ideas on religion, as Leninism coarsened Lenin's own. Lenin had almost a genius for blunt coarseness, and such was his style. To Marx the problem of religion was above all a problem of changing one's thoughts, combined, of course, with the social conflict. To Lenin the problem of religion is almost exclusively a problem of revolutionary conflict and his way of putting the problem was adapted to the needs of this conflict. Lenin summoned men to the 'assault of heaven', but in Lenin's fight against God there is no depth, not the profound motives of Feuerbach and Nietzsche, nothing of what is revealed in Dostoyevsky, no inward drama. Lenin's thoughts on religion which are scattered about in his works were collected together and published separately.(35) One comes across, for instance, such phrases as this: 'Every little god is the lying with a corpse.' Lenin gives his definition of religion and it is rather the definition of a demagogue than of a scientist: 'Religion is one aspect of the spiritual oppression which falls everywhere upon the masses who are condemned to eternal labour for others by their need and their loneliness.' And here is another definition: 'Religion is a sort of spiritual brandy in which the slaves of capital drown the image of their humanity and their demand for some sort of worthy human life.' This definition was made as early as 1905.

Lenin particularly hated any attempt to combine Christianity with socialism. A reforming spirit in the Church was a more harmful thing in his opinion than the Black Hundred. A progressive and regenerated Christianity was worse than the old corrupt Christianity. 'A Roman Catholic priest who seduces a girl', writes Lenin, 'is much less dangerous than a "priest without cassock", a priest without the crudities of religion, an intelligent and democratic priest who preaches the making of some little god or other, for you can expose the first priest, condemn him and get rid of him, but you cannot get rid of the second so easily, and to expose him is a thousand times more difficult.' This category of 'priest without cassock' plays no small part in anti-religious propaganda and it is a category which is very inclusive indeed. 'Priests without cassock' seems to include everyone who is not a materialist, everyone who acknowledges a spiritual principle in life, albeit in the very smallest degree, and all philosophers who are guilty of any spiritual or idealist leanings. Even Einstein was recognized as 'a priest in disguise', because he acknowledged the existence of a cosmic feeling which might be called 'religious'.

Lenin hated the very word 'religion' and he was sharply opposed to regarding socialism as a religion, as Lunacharsky wished to do at one time. Lunacharsky was also a sort of 'priest without cassock', because he preached 'god-construction', which in actual fact was a form of atheism and even militant atheism. But with all Lenin's hatred of religion he was opposed to the policy which would thrust the religious question to the fore and regard the fight against religion as an independent problem, distinct from the revolutionary class struggle. Lenin even spoke against the deliberate insult of religious feelings, though he himself insulted them coarsely. He recommends the reading of French atheist philosophy of the eighteenth century, and this shows how much the atheism of Marx and Lenin depends on the bourgeois enlightenment of that century.

Although the spirit of the eighteenth century enlightened materialism is very powerful in communism still, the Russian communists, who are specialists in anti-religious propaganda, draw a distinction between the radical bourgeois fight against religion in the name of intellectual enlightenment on the one hand and the proletarian revolutionary class struggle against religion on the other. In Soviet anti-religious literature, which is very extensive (for anti-religious propaganda is afforded an honoured position), Plekhanov is reproached on this very ground that he combated religion as a man of enlightenment and, therefore, took up a ridiculously kindly attitude to religion. Plekhánov thought that the spread of enlightenment would lead to the natural dying-out of religious beliefs; religion would disappear of its own accord without any passionate or violent struggle. To Plekhanov it was primarily a question of a change in consciousness, that is to say, a scientific and philosophical question. Against this the Leninists set the revolutionary class struggle, that struggle which inevitably becomes persecution. They continually stress the fact that the fight against religion is not scientific as it was for the men of enlightenment, but a class fight. Such authoritative Western Marxists as Kautsky and Kunov are also explained as men of enlightenment who do not understand revolutionary class war. Kautsky and

Kunov were positivists, not dialectic materialists, that is to say, they were infected with bourgeois radicalism. Kautsky's book *The Origin of Christianity* was very influential in its day in Marxist circles, and use was made of it for anti-religious propaganda in early days in Soviet Russia. The same may be said of Kunov's book *The Origin of Belief in God*. But from the time that the 'general line' was decreed in Soviet philosophy and in anti-religious propaganda, Kautsky's and Kunov's books were rejected and recognized as unsuitable to orthodox Marxist Leninism. Kautsky connects Christianity with a movement of the Roman proletariat. This point of view was recognized as dangerous, since it might suggest to the working class and peasant masses a sympathy for Christianity.

Besides this, Kautsky regarded Christianity less from the point of view of class warfare than as the result of the influence of social environment, that is to say, he tended towards the mechanical not the dialectic explanation, and that is heresy. Kunov was condemned because he made use of the theories of bourgeois scholars, for example, Taylor's *Theory of Animism*, in order to explain the origins of religious beliefs. He was a positivist, not a dialectician. The purpose of anti-religious propaganda required that religion should be regarded simply as a weapon of class oppression; every other point of view on religion is regarded as bourgeois. Only orthodox dialectic materialism provides the one true meaning of the nature of all religion. A young Soviet philosopher wrote a book on the origin of religion from the point of view of Marxist sociology. During a debate in which this book was discussed, the author was attacked in a threatening way because he says nothing in his book about Lenin's views on magic and totemism. With a gesture of despair the author exclaimed that in the whole of Lenin's works there was not a single word about magic or totemism and that he did not know what to do. The bearing of this absurd dialogue is easily understood: the works of Lenin are the Scriptures and in the Scriptures all problems must have been decided beforehand.

The weakest side of Marxism has always been its psychology

[163]

and in Leninism, on account of its prevailing demagogy, psychology is still more weak and crude and elementary. Even the psychology of classes and social groups is not in the least worked out, and its place is taken by elementary moral accusations. Here Leninists are wholly incapable of a clear intellectual position. Their position is merely emotional. So subtle a domain as the field of religious psychology is wholly inaccessible to them. In its anti-religious propaganda Soviet literature stands at a very low intellectual level, and æsthetically its style is intolerable. It is quite the most inferior sort of literature in Soviet Russia. The Soviet anti-religious caricatures are unusually crude, tasteless, and for all their simple directness are but poorly understood by the masses of the people.

A complete methodology is being worked out for the fight against religion. Anti-religious propaganda is imposed as a binding duty upon all Soviet philosophers who are regarded as orthodox, that is to say, who profess the 'general line'. The fight against religion, all religion, enters into the Five Year Plan, which is not only an economic plan but a plan for the complete reconstruction of life. At the same time religious beliefs are recognized as being very much alive among the people, more alive than anything connected with political and economic life, and it is precisely on the religious front that the communists suffer their heaviest defeats. In anti-religious propaganda, what are called religious prejudices and superstitions among the peasants and labouring masses have to be reckoned with. The methods of anti-religious propaganda must take these things into consideration. Can one be a communist, a member of the party, and at the same time a believing Christian? Can one take part in the social programme of communism without sharing the communist world outlook, without being a dialectic materialist and one of the godless? This is a fundamental question.

II

In contrast with the social democrats, the communists do not admit that religion is a private affair and simply a matter for the individual conscience. On the contrary, they consider that religion is one of the most public and social of matters. The recognition of religion as a private affair, that is to say, the recognition of the subjective right to freedom of conscience, is a regular plank in the liberal democratic platform, and this principle is borrowed for social democracy from liberal democracy. Marx himself, having stigmatized religion as 'opium for the people' and the greatest obstacle in the way of securing freedom for the working class and for humanity, could not consider religion a private affair. The question of religion enters into the social struggle. Russian communism draws a logical and extreme deduction from Marx's point of view about religion, a deduction which social democracy was unwilling to draw, because it had absorbed a number of liberal principles. Communists usually called the social democrats 'social traitors', and, by the way, considered them traitors on the religious question. The social democrats, while continuing to consider themselves Marxists, admitted people who were believing Christians to membership of the party, even ministers of religion and professors of theology. But this means that social democracy does not wish to be a 'world outlook'; it wishes to be only a political party, only a system of social reform. I am not speaking of English socialism, which is connected with Christianity far more than with Marxism.

Communism, on the other hand, does want above all to be a 'world outlook'; it is totalitarian and on that account the religious question is very important for it. Russian communism (and, as a matter of fact, communism in general is a Russian creation) builds its whole programme upon a definite 'world outlook'. In Section 13 of the constitution of the communist party, not only the Russian party but also the international, it says that every member of the communist party must be an atheist and carry on anti-religious propaganda. It is required of members of the party that they break off every kind of relation with the Church. Lenin clearly established the principles by which the communist must be controlled in his relation to religion. He expounded in what sense religion may be considered a private affair; religion is a private affair in relation to a bourgeois state; in a bourgeois state the communist must stand for freedom of conscience, for the separation of the Church from the State, must defend the principle that religion is a private affair. But the whole argument changes when it is a question of the relation of religion to the communist party and consequently in a communist state and society. Religion is certainly not a private affair within the communist party. It is then the most public and the most social of matters; then a merciless fight against religion becomes necessary. The communist, the real integral communist, cannot be a religious man, a believing man; he cannot be a Christian. A definite world outlook is binding upon a member of the communist party; he must be a materialist and an atheist, and, what is more, a militant atheist. It is not enough to share in the socialist programme of communism to make one a member of the communist party; communism is the profession of a definite faith, a faith which is opposed to Christianity. All Soviet literature asserts such an interpretation of communism. Communists are fond of emphasizing that they are opponents of Christian evangelical morality based upon love, pity, and sympathy, and that perhaps is the most dreadful thing in communism.

On opportunist grounds an exception is made in the case of the workers in this matter of religion. Since there still exist among the working classes traces of religious prejudices, those who cling to them may still be accepted into the communist party if they share the social programme of communism, without making enquiries about their religious beliefs, but in the case of members of the intelligentsia this is not permissible. The story of the Swedish communist Hedlund, is very characteristic. He endeavoured to assert that religion is a matter for every man's conscience and that it is possible to be a communist as well as a believing Christian. Hedlund was very sharply attacked for this, and subjected to very severe treatment by Yaroslavsky (36), the chief specialist in antireligious propaganda. It was explained to him that within the ranks of communism religion is not considered a private affair. At the present time a member of the communist party cannot attend church or profess religious belief of any sort; more than that, he places himself under suspicion if he shows any coolness in anti-religious propaganda and does not profess militant communism. In its very make-up and in the spiritual structure of its adepts, the communist party is something in the nature of an atheist sect, a religious atheist sect which has got the Government into its hands.

It is idle to suppose that the religious persecution in Russia is directed only against the Orthodox Church, which was the dominant church and associated in the past with monarchy and reaction. Sects, for instance the Baptists, are regarded as still more dangerous than the Orthodox, and the struggle against them is regarded as more difficult, just because in the past it was they who were persecuted by, and not associated with, the authorities of the old régime. Christians who recognize the justice of communism in the domain of social life, are considered more harmful and dangerous than Christians who are openly in favour of restoration of the old social order and engage in counter-revolutionary activity. A free-thinking, atheist and materialist bourgeoisie is to be preferred to Christians who sympathize with communism; it can be used for the socialist work of construction; it is usually indifferent to the question of a 'general outlook', whereas the Christian communists make a breach in the integral wholeness of the communist 'world outlook'. It was Lenin who made this pronouncement.(37)

Religious persecution is not recommended in the handbooks devoted to anti-religious propaganda, and Yaroslavsky, the specialist on godlessness, says there is nothing gained by making martyrs, but in actual fact they do make martyrs. Priests are reduced to existence under inhuman conditions; they are *lishentsi,* 'deprived' of the most elementary human rights, pariahs in the Soviet State. It is clearly desired to place ministers of religions in such a position that they cannot exist. The material and moral position of priests, against whom no charge of any sort has been brought, is intolerable, so that sometimes they prefer to be put into prison. But besides all this, bishops and priests are continually being arrested, exiled to Solovky and shot. Communists who go to church are excluded from the party. Soviet employés are dismissed if they go to church; they can attend church only in secret, somewhere on the outskirts of the town. To profess one's faith openly in Soviet

Russia calls for heroism and frequently involves martyrdom. The priest may speak about God only in church in his professional capacity; outside church he is forbidden to speak about Him. Freedom of conscience, of course, does not exist in Soviet Russia. The Soviet constitution, which separated the Church from the State and proclaimed freedom of conscience, has no meaning whatever. Coercion is not only a matter of practice, it enters into the theoretical world outlook of communism; it is part of its teaching. Representatives of the Soviet Government, when they are spoken to about anti-religious persecution, commonly reply that there is no such persecution, that they persecute solely the counter-revolutionaries of which there are very many among the bishops and priests and the believing laity, and that the Church is persecuted only in so far as it is the home of reaction and counter-revolution. But this diplomatic explanation is contradicted by the fact that in all their writings which set out their general point of view and their own faith, the communists demand a militant conflict against all religion. They will say that this conflict is in the realm of ideas and takes place in thought, and this was the view that Marx took of the fight against religion. But this is a purely theoretical argument.

The really important thing is that now the Russian communists represent the Government. The State is in their hands, and this State belongs to the period of dictatorship, a dictatorship of world view, a dictatorship which is not only political and economic but also intellectual, a dictatorship over spirit, conscience and thought. This dictatorship makes no bones about the means it employs; it employs all means. This state of affairs is an ideocracy; it is one of the transformations of the platonic Utopia. It is this which makes the denial of freedom of conscience and thought inevitable, and makes inevitable religious persecution. All controversies in the sphere of theory, ideas and philosophy, and all disputes in the practical, political and economic world in Soviet Russia, are fought out under the banners of orthodoxy and heresy. All those who incline to the 'right' or to the 'left' in philosophy or in politics are regarded as inclined to heresy; and the exposure of heretics and the persecution of those convicted of heresy is continually taking place. But the distinction between orthodoxy and heresy is a religious, a theological distinction, it is not philosophical and political. When politics are placed under the banner of an orthodoxy, then the State is regarded as a Church, and persecution on the ground of faith and opinion cannot be avoided. Christian theocracy in the Middle Ages was like this, and so is the Soviet communist 'theocracy', so is Hitler's Third Reich, and so is every state which professes to be totalitarian. I have already said that Ivan the Terrible, the most notable exponent of the theory of autocracy, founded the conception of an Orthodox Tsardom in which the salvation of the souls of his subjects was one of the duties of the Tsar. The functions of the Church are transferred to the State. The communist government also is concerned for the salvation of the souls of its subjects; it desires to bring them up in the one saving truth; it knows the truth, the truth of dialectic materialism. The communist government, which is an unlimited government, finds its motive power in hatred of Christianity, in which it sees the cause of slavery, exploitation and darkness of mind.

The communists are extraordinarily ignorant and unenlightened in religious matters. But they are controlled by motives which belong to the world of ideas; they are inspired by their own religious faith. The communist government not infrequently displays a great pliancy in politics. It can be very opportunist in international politics and make concessions in economic politics. It is even ready to grant a certain liberty in art and literature. Communism is changing; it is developing; it is becoming nationalized, and more cultured. Communist life is becoming bourgeois, and this last process constitutes a great danger not for communism alone, but also for the Russian idea in the world. But there is a domain in which communism is changeless, pitiless, fanatical and in which it will grant no concessions whatever. That is the domain of 'world outlook', of philosophy and consequently of religion also. Soviet philosophical literature as a whole, and its literature concerned with anti-religious propaganda in particular, is most unenlightened most fanatical and stereotyped. The dogmatism of this literature exceeds anything that has occurred in Christian theology. It sometimes looks as though the Soviet government would rather go on to the restoration of capitalism in economic life than to granting freedom of conscience, freedom of philosophic thought, freedom to create a spiritual culture. This hatred for religion and Christianity has its roots deep down in the past of Christianity.

III

The hatred which the Russian communists feel for Christianity involves a self-contradiction which those whose judgment is subjected by communist doctrine are not in a position to observe. The best type of communist, that is to say, the man who is completely in the grip of the service of an idea and capable of enormous sacrifices and disinterested enthusiasm, is a possibility only as the result of the Christian training of the human spirit, of the remaking of the natural man by the Christian spirit. The result of this Christian influence upon the human spirit, frequently hidden and unperceived, remains even when the people consciously refuse Christianity, and even become its foe. If it were granted that anti-religious propaganda were finally to destroy all traces of Christianity in the soul of the Russian people, and annihilate all religious feeling, then the actual realization of communism would become impossible, for no one would be willing to make sacrifices, no one would interpret life as service of a higher purpose, and the final victory would remain with the self-seeking type who thinks only of his own interests. This last type of person, even now, already plays no small part, and the growth of the bourgeois spirit is due to him.

According to its own ideas communism desires the existence not only of righteousness but also of brotherhood in human relations, a communism among men, but it is absurd and ridiculous to suppose that the brotherhood of man can be realized by the external coercion of social regimentation, by growing accustomed to it, as Lenin says; it requires the action of profound spiritual forces. Materialist and atheist communism is either doomed to fail and perish or is bound to establish a society which is like a mechanism

[170]

in which the human form can no longer be distinguished. None the less the communists, indebted as they are in many ways to Christianity, basing—as they do—their whole activity upon the switching over of religious energy, that is to say, the application of it to something which is not religious, hate Christianity and religion in general.

There must be deep and serious causes for this, causes which cannot be simply due to the profession of an abstract theory of hostility to religion. Christians, who condemn the communists for their godlessness and anti-religious persecutions, cannot lay the whole blame solely upon these godless communists; they must assign part of the blame to themselves, and that a considerable part. They must be not only accusers and judges; they must also be penitents. Have Christians done very much for the realization of Christian justice in social life? Have they striven to realize the brotherhood of man without that hatred and violence of which they accuse the communists? The sins of Christians, the sins of the historical churches, have been very great, and these sins bring with them their just punishment. Betrayal of the covenant of Christ, the use of the Christian Church for the support of the ruling classes, human weakness being what it is, cannot but bring about the lapse from Christianity of those who are compelled to suffer from that betrayal and from such a distortion of Christianity. In the Prophets, in the Gospels, in the Apostolic Epistles, in most of the Doctors of the Church, we find censure of the riches of the rich and repudiation of property, and the affirmation of the equality of all men before God. In Basil the Great, and especially in John Chrysostom, may be met judgments upon social injustice due to wealth and property, so sharp that Proudhon and Marx pale before them. The Doctors of the Church said that property is theft. St. John Chrysostom was a complete communist, though of course his was not communism of the capitalist or the industrial period. There are good grounds for asserting that communism has Christian or Judaic-Christian origins.(38) But there soon came a time in which Christianity was adapted to the contemporary kingdom of Cæsar. The discovery was made that Christianity is not only the truth with which the world may be set aflame, but that it might be socially useful for the establishment of the kingdom of Cæsar. Christians—hierarchs, bishops, priests—set about defending the ruling classes, the rich, and the powerful. False inferences were drawn from the doctrine of original sin to justify every existing evil and injustice. Suffering and trial were recognized as useful for the salvation of the soul, and this was applied chiefly to the oppressed classes, doomed to suffering and hardship, and was not applied to the oppressor and the violent. Christian humility was falsely interpreted and this interpretation used for the denial of human worth and for the demand of meek submission to every social evil. Christianity was used to justify the humiliation of man and to defend oppression.

It must always be remembered that the Church bears two different meanings, and the confusion of these two meanings or the denial of one of them has fatal results. The Church is the mystical Body of Christ, a spiritual reality, continuing in history the Life of Christ, and its origin is revelation, the action of God upon man and the world. But the Church is also a social phenomenon, a social institution; it is linked with its social environment, and feels its influence; it finds itself in interaction with the State; it has its own law and polity and its origin is social. The Church as a social institution, as part of history, is sinful, liable to fall and to distort the eternal truth of Christianity, passing off the temporary and human as the eternal and divine. The Church in history is a very complex divine-human and not only divine process, and the human side of it is fallible; but the eternal truth of the Church of Christ acts secretly and operates through the Church as a social institution which is always relative and fallible. The Marxist-Leninists see the Church only as a social phenomenon and institution and see nothing behind it. To them the whole is thrust into the foreground; to them there is no spiritual life; that is only an epiphenomenon. Existence is flat, two-dimensional; there is no measurement of depth. But communism must be understood as a challenge to the Christian world. In it is to be seen the Highest Tribunal and a reminder of duty unfulfilled. The communists themselves do not understand this and cannot understand it. The communists expose the evil violent actions of Christians but they themselves continue to do the same evil and violence. Their responsibility may be less because they do not know the truth of Christianity, but they are responsible for the fact that they do not desire to know it.

There are two very significant books by Hecker published in English. (39) They convey a very hazy impression. If Hecker simply defended communism and the communist point of view all would be clear, but his attitude to Christianity is different from that of a thorough-going communist and, probably on account of his own past, he would like to preserve a certain value in Christianity, though one which sets him in sharp contradiction to the Christianity of the Church. His attitude to Christianity reminds one of that of the rationalist-moralist type of sectarian. Everything that Hecker says about Christianity witnesses to the fact that he entirely fails to see and understand the mystical side of it. To him the Church is simply a social phenomenon, defined by its environment and infected with all the ills of the ruling classes in history; he is incapable of recognizing the spiritual side of it. Religion he derives from fear which was afterwards sublimated. He explains it in a purely sociological sense. Hecker regards it as undoubted that man is descended from a simian ancestor, that is to say, that he has an animal origin. In conformity with the philosophy which is dominant and obligatory in Soviet Russia, he takes, of course, the dialectic point of view, although no traces are to be seen in him of the assimilation of Hegelianism. In the Orthodox Church Hecker sees only its outward side (ceremonies behind which, of course, he sees no mysteries), the link with the monarchist state and slavish dependence upon it, and the subservience of the clergy. Hecker's exclusive this-worldliness does not allow him any feeling for the theme of salvation and eternal life. The value of Christianity for him is simply a matter of ethics and the organization of social life. Orthodoxy appears to him as a form of Christianity which has not evolved any system of ethics as its own and exerts no influence for the betterment of social life. The problem of religion appears to him to be finally subordinate to the social use which he can make of it, and therefore the question of its truth does not arise. This is Anglo-Saxon pragmatism—a thing which is readily perceived in Hecker and which in actual fact contradicts the communists' general outlook, which claims the knowledge of absolute truth.

Hecker is the apologist of Russian communism to the West, but he is certainly not a thorough-going communist; his general outlook is eclectic. Hecker is an admirer of Leo Tolstoi and apparently is disposed to understand Christianity as L. Tolstoi understood it, that is to say, principally as an ethical code. This is the result of Hecker's sectarian Christianity. I am myself disposed to think that L. Tolstoi was the awakener of the Christian conscience in a torpid Christian world and that there was much truth in his criticism of historical Christianity. I have already said that there were elements of Russian nihilism in L. Tolstoi which make him one of the forerunners of Russian communism, but it is impossible to deduce from this, as apparently Hecker is inclined to do, that communism realizes Tolstoi's ideas. Communist ideology and especially its practice are diametrically opposed to the teaching of Tolstoi. Communism represents the extreme of violent resistance, extreme *étatism*, the lure of technical civilization and industry, the denial of the essential brotherhood of man, the disruption of immediate links with the soil, the destruction of the religious principle of life. L. Tolstoi taught non-resistance, an anarchic repudiation of the State and of technical civilization, the acknowledgement of the essential brotherhood of man, links with the soil and the affirmation of the religious principle of life.

In his attacks upon the past of the Orthodox Church in Russia, Hecker is frequently true in his facts. Nothing is easier than to show that the history of the Church and in general the history of Christianity is to a considerable degree a history of human sin, treachery, decadence and subservience in despite of conscience. From the time of Constantine the Church has not so much mastered the kingdom of Cæsar as been subjected to it. The history of religion as linked with its social environment, with social claims and interests, has always been more prominent and more powerful than the history of religion as linked with revelation and the spiritual life. But it is only spiritual weakness and blindness, only the subjugation of the spirit to its outward environment, which leads from that to the conclusion that there is no such thing as revelation and no such thing as the spiritual world.

There is no doubt that the Church, as a social institution, was in a state of subjection in Russia and even enslaved by the State. The degrading dependence of the Church upon the State belonged not only to the time of Peter but also to the Muscovite period. It is even indisputable that the clergy in Russia were in a degraded and dependent position and that they lost all sense of leadership especially from the time of the schism. The level of the episcopate was particularly low; the bishops who, during the period of the Tartar yoke and to some extent the Muscovite period, had a sense of spiritual leadership, became civil servants, governors, the recipients of stars and ribands, and drove in their carriages. The bishops usually persecuted the *Startsi,* that is to say, men who were specially spiritual, and every spontaneous manifestation of religious life. Corresponding facts are to be seen in the Roman Catholic Church too. It is incontestable that in the Revolution the Orthodox Church has to pay for the sins of its past. Church people cannot suddenly repudiate the links of the historical Church with the old régime. But to see all this does not justify the hangman; and the protest against the slavish subjection of the Church in the old kingdom of Cæsar certainly cannot lead to the demand for slavish subjection to a new kingdom of Cæsar, although this may call itself communist. With all the actual truth to fact of much that Hecker says about Orthodoxy, and that might be said of the past of Catholicism and Protestantism, his general judgments are mistaken and entirely out of perspective; and this is inevitable since for Hecker spirit and spiritual life do not exist. In his view the Orthodox Church amounts to no more than outward formality, faith in ceremonial and relics of old superstitions. His sympathies are only with the rationalist sects. But what has acted upon the Russian soul and moulded it is the hidden spiritual life of Orthodoxy, not outward official ecclesiasticism. It is useless for Hecker to regard the liturgical life of the Church as mere outward formality, as something in the nature of superstitious magic, when in fact spiritual depth and the reflection of heavenly life exist in it. Khomyakov's teaching about the Church, that is to say, his teaching about *sobornost*[1] and freedom, seems to Hecker a Utopia which has never been realized in actual fact, simply because to his mind reality is exhausted by empirical data; and he is incapable of understanding a world of ideas in the ontological sense behind the empirical world and opposed to it even while it acts upon it. Therefore he sees in the Church only a crude empiricism and does not see its ideal form, that is to say, the mystical Body of Christ.

All Russian creative religious thought of the nineteenth and twentieth centuries, beginning with Khomyakov and the Slavophils down to the thinkers of the beginning of the twentieth, censured the sins of the historical Church of Russia, and frequently spoke more sharply than Hecker; the statement that the Russian Church was paralysed belongs to Dostoyevsky the Orthodox Christian. Neither Russian communism nor Hecker's books are required to show the humiliating falsity of the relation which existed between the Church and the old state. This was frequently referred to very severely by men who were believers and even considered themselves supporters of the monarchy—Khomyakov, Samarin, Aksakov, Dostoyevsky, Solovëv and many others. Russian creative religious thought, from Khomyakov onwards, had entered upon the path of religious reformation within Orthodoxy. Indictments of the spiritual hierarchy, and especially of the episcopate, are very commonly found among those representatives of Orthodoxy who have nothing in common with sectarianism. Not only the sectarians but also those Russian religious thinkers to whom Hecker is disposed to ascribe no significance whatever, were distinguished by a certain nonconformity. But Hecker says nothing about the immense and beneficial part played by the Church in social life during the Tartar period, or about the love of the poor in ancient Russia. He makes no reference to the positive

[1]See footnote on p. 87.

phenomena of Russian sainthood. He does not understand that Russian Orthodoxy, alien though it is from moralism, was in the last resort that which gave their inward training to the souls of those too whose minds have abandoned it, and which evoked in the souls of the Russian people the search for the Kingdom of God and His righteousness, and which brought into being that humanity and sympathy which are so widely reflected in Russian literature. Hecker does not understand that if real marks of saintliness were to be found in Chernishevsky, marks of the *podvizhnik*,[1] he derived them from the Christianity of his childhood and youth. Decadence in the official Church and weakening of Christian life among the people preceded the revolution. And so it always happens. Formal Orthodoxy frequently presented a horrible appearance. At the beginning of the twentieth century a religious renaissance took place in a very restricted circle in Russia, and it was a phenomenon belonging not so much to popular life as to a cultured *élite*. For that reason, as I have said already, it was ineffective socially. Rasputin was a symbol of the disintegration of the old world and evidence of the spiritual inevitability of revolution; but Hecker's understanding and appraisement of the whole Russian religious–philosophical movement is too inaccurate, and after all he cannot class it with official State Orthodoxy.

In the first place, Hecker uses the term 'the search for God incorrectly; it is not applicable to currents of thought which regarded themselves definitely as Christian. Speaking of the 'neo-Christians' (a permissible term as long as one is speaking of Christians who believe in the possibility of a new creative epoch in Christianity), Hecker reckons amongst them V. Rozanov who was undoubtedly a thinker of genius, but was a definite foe of Christianity and may rather be called a neo-pagan. Many inaccuracies of statement might be pointed out in Hecker. He looks at those spiritual phenomena which he is writing about, from a distance; his judgments are too sweeping; he has no light and shade, no appreciation of individual characteristics. Moreover, it must be pointed out that everyone who adheres to the philosophy

[1]One who performs great exploits in the ascetic life; a spiritual 'athlete'.

of communism loses the ability to distinguish the individual thing.

What Hecker finally and hopelessly fails to understand is the problem of personality in Christian consciousness. Defence of the principle of personality he apparently identifies with individualism and egoism. He seems to think that when the Gospel calls upon a man to lay down his life for his friend it is declaring against the principle of personality. But the recognition of the absolute value of every personality as made in the image and likeness of God, the inadmissibility of treating the human personality as a mere instrument or tool, lies at the very basis of Christianity. It is precisely Christianity which teaches that the human soul is of more value than all the kingdoms of the world. Christianity pays endless attention to every individual man and to his individual fate. A human being, always individual and never to be repeated, is for Christianity a more primary and deep reality than society. A man may and frequently ought to sacrifice his life but not his personality; the personality within him he ought to realize, and sacrifice is the condition of realizing personality. It is personality which is called to eternal life, which is the conquest of eternity. Personality is a spiritual-religious category and indicates the task which is set before men. Personality is an entirely different thing from the individuum, which is a biological and sociological category and the subordinate part of the family and the community. Personality cannot be a part of anything, neither of the community nor of the world; it is an entirety and in virtue of its depth it belongs to the spiritual world and not to the natural.(40) All the limitation and falsity of communist philosophy is due to the failure to understand the problem of personality, and this turns communism into a dehumanizing power hostile to man; it takes the community, the socialist community, a social class, the proletariat, and makes it into an idol, and the real human being is denied and rejected.

I ought to say a word or two about Hecker's false interpretation of my own views. The terminology which I use, the words 'aristocratic principle', 'the new Middle Ages', etc., clearly lead him astray. He regards me as a supporter of feudal aristocracy, which is almost laughable. A supporter of feudal aristocracy in our day would have to be regarded as mad. In actual fact, I am a supporter of the classless society, that is to say, in that respect I am very near to communism. (41) But for all that, I am a supporter of the aristocratic principle as a qualitative principle in human society, but a personal qualitative principle, not one which depends upon class or property; that is to say, I am a supporter of spiritual aristocracy. Class inequality ought to be overcome in human society, but personal inequality would come out all the stronger for that. Man should be distinguished from man by his personal quality not by his social position, his class or his property. The qualitative, that is to say, the personal aristocratic principle, cannot disappear from human society. On the contrary, it will become all the clearer in a classless society, when classes no longer exist, for classes mask and conceal personal qualitative differences among men and make them symbolic, not real. A man occupies a high position in the community not on the strength of his personal qualities and his spiritual aristocracy, but symbolically, in virtue of what is conferred upon him by his belonging to a certain class. I am a supporter of Christian personalism, certainly not of individualism which is hostile to the principle of personality. In a bourgeois capitalist community personality is levelled down and is looked upon merely as an atom. (42) Individualism is hostile to the Christian idea of the communion of men, whereas the realization of personality presupposes the communion of men.

When I say that the world is moving towards a new Middle Ages, I certainly do not mean a return to the old Middle Ages and least of all to feudalism. The phrase is only an indication of the type of society in which man will strive after wholeness and unity as opposed to the individualism of modern history, and in which the significance of the religious principle will increase, even though it may be in the form of militant anti-religion. Hecker also completely fails to understand the new problems of Russian religious thought. These problems, while not sundering the links with the inward spiritual tradition of the Orthodox Church, are concerned with creative efforts in the Christian world. The problem of Christian anthropology is sharply stated and, in connection with it, the problem of Christian culture and Christian society. Russian creative religious thought has introduced the idea of God-humanity. As in Jesus Christ, the God-Man, there occurred an individual incarnation of God in man, so similarly in humanity there should occur a collective incarnation of God. God-humanity is the continuation of the incarnation of God; it brings forward the problem of the incarnation of the truth and righteousness of Christ in the life of humanity, in human culture and human society The idea of God-humanity as the essence of Christianity is but little developed in Western Christian thought; it is an original product of Russian Christian thought, in which Christian philosophy is understood as the philosophy of God-humanity, as christological. It passes beyond the boundaries of Greek and scholastic thought as well as those of the rationalist thought of modern times. This whole sphere is completely alien to Hecker who does not understand it at all. As a pragmatist and social utilitarian he judges the significance and value of a phenomenon of spirit and thought solely by its immediate social effect. But there can be very effective movements in the world which are completely hostile to spirit and thought, when man is thrust wholly into the outward side of things and achieves aims which are perhaps important but other than the deeper aims of spirit and thought. The problems of Russian religious thought are concerned with the more distant future when the pressing economic questions have been decided; its orientation is towards eternity.

Hecker takes the so-called 'Living Church' under his protection and he assigns it, of course, a clear primacy over the Patriarchal Orthodox Church. It seems to him, as it has seemed to many in the West, that the movement of the 'Living Church' is something in the nature of a Reformation, that it is akin to Protestantism. This is a mistake. There was no sort of reformation movement in Russia at the time of the revolution, though there was among the clergy at the very beginning of the twentieth century. The leaders of the 'Living Church', which has now lost all significance, were devoid of any religious creative idea. It was a mere self-adjustment by a part of the Orthodox clergy to the existing government; it was not reformation but conformism. There the traditions of the old slavery of the Church hierarchy to State authority made themselves heard. Apart from other considerations the adherents of the 'Living Church' are unworthy of any respect because they became informers against the Patriarch and the hierarchs of the Patriarchal Church, they became ecclesiastical spies and adjusted themselves to those who held power. They were linked with the G.P.U. which issued its instructions to the 'Living Church'. This revived the old relation between Church and State, the Procurator being a member of the G.P.U. No fundamental reforming movement of any sort ever arose from compliance and subservience, from delation and spying; such movements have arisen when those who spoke for them sacrificed themselves, not others.

The 'Living Church' movement had no religious ideas of any sort; it said nothing but that the Church ought to adapt itself to the Soviet Government, but that is not a religious idea. Its adherents did not rise even to the idea that there is Christian truth in communism; they were interested not in communism but in the Government. I myself hold much more radical ideas than the adherents of the 'Living Church' and I believe more than they do in the new creative ideas of Christianity, in the new outpouring of the Holy Spirit upon man. But I am utterly opposed to the 'Living Church' because I consider that sort of conformism in religious life is inadmissible. The Orthodox Church in Russia ought to establish some sort of *concordat* with the existing government, as the Metropolitan Sergius is trying to do. The Church cannot occupy itself in political strife, and all suspicion of connection with the old régime ought to be removed from it. But the Church must rise above the kingdom of Cæsar. A condemnation by the Church of the capitalist régime, its recognition of the justice of socialism and of a labouring community, would in my opinion be very right, but under the Soviet régime it loses all religious meaning, for it becomes the mere carrying out of the demands of the G.P.U.

IV

We now approach the fundamental problem of communism, the problem of the relation between man and society. Hecker shares all the weaknesses of the communist statement and the communist solution of this problem, that is to say, for him the problem of man has no dimension of depth. What was the case with Marx? Marx was an admirable sociologist but a very feeble anthropologist. Marxism states the problem of society but not that of man. In its view man is a function of society, a technical function of economics. Society is the phenomenon, while man is the epiphenomenon. Such a degrading of man is a striking contradiction to the accusatory teaching of Marx about the *verdinglichung* of human life and about dehumanization. There remains in him a rooted duality of thought: Is the turning of man into a function of the economic process a sin and an evil of past capitalist exploitation or is it the ontology of man? In any case, the fact is decisive that the first attempt to realize communism on Marxist soil which we see in Russia also regards man as a function of economics and also dehumanizes human life as the capitalist régime does. Therefore, no such revolution in world history as Marx and Engels hoped for has taken place.

Meanwhile, communism claims to have created not only the new society but also the new man. They talk a great deal in Soviet Russia about the new man, about a new spiritual make-up. Foreigners who have visited Soviet Russia are also fond of talking about it; but the new man can only come into being in the event of man being regarded as of supreme value in life. If man is considered simply as a brick in the structure of society, if he is but an instrument in the economic process, then one must speak not so much of the appearance of the new man as of the disappearance of man, that is to say, of the intensifying of the process of dehumanization. Man is deprived of the measurement of depth; he is turned into a flat two-dimensioned being. The new man will exist only if he has a measurement of depth, if he is a spiritual being; otherwise man does not exist; he is but a function of the community. In his dimension of depth, man is a sharer not only in time but in eternity.

If man is wholly relegated to the time process, if nothing of eternity and for eternity exists in him, then the image of man, the image of personality, cannot be preserved. In its atheistic materialist form communism entirely subordinates man to the time process; man is only a transient unit in a series of moments and every moment is but the means which produces the next. Thus man loses his interior existence; human life is dehumanized. Marxism revealed a crisis in humanism. In Marx, especially during his younger days, when he still kept traces of German idealism, there were possibilities of a new humanism; he began with a revolt against dehumanization, but later he himself was influenced by the process of dehumanization, and in relation to man communism inherited the sins of capitalism.

In Russian Marxist communism this process of dehumanization went even further and was conditioned by the whole set of circumstances in which Russian communism arose. There entered into Russian communism the traditions not of Russian humanism, which had a Christian origin, but of Russian anti-humanism, deriving from Russian state absolutism, which always regarded man as a mere means to an end. Marxism considers evil as the pathway to good. The new society, the new man, is born of the growth of evil and darkness; the soul of the new man is formed by negative emotions, by hatred, revenge and violence. This is the demoniacal element of Marxism and it is called dialectic. Dialectically, evil passes over into good, darkness into light. Lenin proclaimed that everything was moral which served the proletarian revolution. He knows no other definition of good. From this it follows that the end justifies the means, every sort of means. The moral impulse in human life loses all independent significance, and that is undoubted dehumanization. The end for the sake of which every means is justified is not man, not the new man, not the completeness of humanity, but only a new organization of society. Man is a means for this new organization of society and not the new organization of society for man.

The communist is defined psychologically chiefly by the fact that for him the world is sharply divided into two opposed camps

[183]

—Ormuzd and Ahriman, the kingdom of light and the kingdom of darkness, without any shading. This is almost a Manichæan dualism which at the same time commonly makes use of a monist doctrine. The kingdom of the proletariat is the light kingdom of Ormuzd; the kingdom of the bourgeoisie is the dark kingdom of Ahriman. To those who belong to the kingdom of light everything is permissible for the annihilation of the kingdom of darkness. The fanaticism, intolerance, cruelty and violence of the thorough-going type of communist is explained by the fact that he feels himself faced by the kingdom of Satan and he cannot endure that kingdom. But at the same time he depends negatively upon the kingdom of Satan, upon evil, upon capitalism, upon the bourgeoisie. He cannot live without an enemy, without the feeling of hostility to that enemy; he loses his *pathos* when that enemy does not exist, and if there is no enemy he must invent one. The prosecutions of 'saboteurs' are due to this requirement of creating a class enemy. If the class enemy finally disappeared and communism easily existed the communist *pathos* would also disappear. The revolutionary *pathos* is to a large extent due to a hostile attitude to the past. The question is sometimes put: To what extent does communism actually belong to the future and is it concerned with the future? Undoubtedly it is more concerned with the future than is fascism, which is an entirely transitional phenomenon. A world problem is connected with communism; but in communism there is too great a dependence upon the past, a falling in love with hatred of the past; it is too much shackled to the evil of capitalism and the bourgeoisie. Communism cannot conquer hate, and in that lies its chief weakness. Hatred always turns to the past and always depends upon the past. A man who is gripped by the emotion of hatred cannot be concerned with the future, with a new life; only love turns a man towards the future, frees him from the heavy shackles of the past, and is a means of creating a new and better life. The preponderance of hate over love is terrible among communists. One cannot entirely blame them for this. In that respect they are victims of past evil.

The spirit of communism, the religion of communism, the

philosophy of communism, are both anti-Christian and anti-humanist. But the social system of communism possesses a large share of truth which can be wholly reconciled with Christianity, more so, in any case, than the capitalist system, which is most anti-Christian, Communism is right as against capitalism. The falsity of the communist spirit and of its spiritual servitude can be condemned only by those Christians who cannot be suspected of defending 'the interests of the bourgeois capitalist world. It is precisely the capitalist system above all which crushes personality and dehumanizes human life, turns man into a thing and an article of merchandise; and it does not become the defenders of this system to condemn communists for repudiating human personality and dehumanizing human life. It was the industrial capitalist period which subjected man to the power of economics and money, and it does not become its adepts to teach communists the evangelical truth that man does not live by bread alone. The question of bread for myself is a material question, but the question of bread for my neighbours, for everybody, is a spiritual and a religious question. Man does not live by bread alone, but he does live by bread and there should be bread for all. Society should be so organized that there is bread for all, and then it is that the spiritual question will present itself before men in all its depth. It is not permissible to base a struggle for spiritual interests and for a spiritual renaissance on the fact that for a considerable part of humanity bread will not be guaranteed. Such cynicism as this justly evokes an atheistic reaction and the denial of spirit. Christians ought to be permeated with a sense of the religious importance of the elementary daily needs of men, the vast masses of men, and not to despise these needs from the point of view of an exalted spirituality.

Communism is a great mentor for Christians; it is a frequent reminder to them of Christ and the Gospels and of the prophetic elements in Christianity. In regard to economic life two contradictory principles may be postulated. One of them says: In economic life follow up your own personal interest and this will promote the economic development of the whole, it will be good for the community, for the nation, for the state. Such is the bourgeois ideology of economics. The other principle says: In economic life serve others, serve the whole community and then you will receive everything which you need for your life. Communism asserts this second principle, and in that respect it is right. It is abundantly clear that the second principle corresponds to Christianity more closely than the first. The first principle is just as anti-Christian as the Roman theory of property. Bourgeois political economy, having invented the economic man and eternal economic laws, regards the second principle as utopian. But the economic man is transient, and a new motive for labour is entirely possible, a motive which corresponds more with the value of a man. One thing is clear: this problem cannot be only a problem of a new organization of society. It is inevitably a problem of a new make-up of man, of a new man. But the new man cannot be prepared in mechanical ways; he cannot be the automatic result of a certain organization of society. A new spiritual make-up presupposes a re-training of man spiritually. To this last problem communism is obliged to devote much attention, but it does not possess the spiritual strength for solving it. It is impossible to create the new man and the new society while proclaiming that economic life is a function which concerns civil servants alone. This is not the socialization of economics, but their bureaucratization.

Communism in the form in which it has appeared in Russia is extreme *étatism*; it is the appearing of the monster Leviathan which has laid its paws upon everything. The Soviet Government, as I have already said, is the one totalitarian state in the world which is carried to its logical consistent end; it is a transformation of the ideas of Ivan the Terrible, a new form of the terrible hypertrophy of the state in Russian history. But to understand economic life as social service certainly does not mean the conversion of every economic agent into a civil servant, nor the recognition of the state as the only economic agent. It is indisputable that a part of commerce, of commerce on the most considerable scale, ought to pass over to the state. But side by side with this one must recognize the co-operation of men, the labouring syndicate, and the separate man established by the organization of society in conditions which exclude the exploitation of one's neighbour; and the state will have controlling and mediating functions, such as will not permit the oppression of man by man. It does not enter within the scope of my present task to go into the details of these questions; only it is important to notice that *étatism* is not the only form of the new organization of society. The pluralist rather than the monist social system corresponds more truly with the freedom of the human spirit. The monist social system always leads to tyranny and the oppression of human personality; the monism of the Marxist system is its principal defect. The monism of a totalitarian state is in any case incompatible with Christianity; it turns the state into a Church, and a heroic conflict is in store against the absolute claims of the kingdom of Cæsar in communism and in fascism. During this struggle Christianity may be cleansed and freed from the stamp of the kingdom of Cæsar which has lain upon the Church since the time of Constantine. Christianity seems to me to be compatible only with a system which I would call a system of pluralist socialism, which unites the principle of personality as the supreme value, with the principle of a brotherly community of men. At the same time it is necessary to make a distinction, which the communists do not make, between the realization of righteousness in the life of the community, presupposing the impulse of coercion, and the realization of the brotherhood of men, of their true community or communion, presupposing the freedom of man and the action of grace.

In this book I have tried to show that Russian communism is more traditional than is commonly thought and that it is a transformation and deformation of the old Russian messianic idea. Communism in Western Europe would be an entirely different phenomenon in spite of the similarity of Marxist theories. To the traditional Russian character of communism are due both its positive and its negative sides: On the one hand the search for the Kingdom of God and integrated truth and justice, capacity for sacrifice and the absence of the bourgeois spirit; on the other hand, the absoluteness of the State, and despotism, a feeble grasp of the rights of man and the danger of a featureless collectivism. In other countries communism, in the event of an attempt to bring it into existence, may be less integrated, make less claim to take the place of religion, may be more secular and more bourgeois in its spirit. The problems of communism stimulate the awakening of the Christian conscience and should lead to the development of a creative social Christianity, not in the sense of understanding Christianity as a social religion, but in the sense of revealing Christian truth and justice in relation to social life. This will mean emancipation from social slavery, that social slavery in which Christian consciousness finds itself. The world is living through the danger of a dehumanization of social life, the dehumanization of man himself. The very existence of man is in danger from all the processes which are going on in the world. Only the spiritual strengthening of man can combat this danger. When Christianity appeared in the world it defended man from the danger arising from demonolatry. Man was in the power of cosmic forces, of demons and spirits of Nature which tormented him. Christianity focused man spiritually and subjected his fate to God; thus was prepared the possibility of man's power over Nature. At the present time Christianity is again called upon to protect man, to protect his whole image from a demonolatry which torments him anew, from servitude to the old cosmic and the new technical forces. But this can only be done by a rejuvenated Christianity which is true to its prophetic spirit and which is turned towards the Kingdom of God.

AUTHOR'S NOTES

(1) Page 8. See the interesting book: *Das Antlitz Russlands und das Gesicht der Revolution,* by Fedor Stepan.

(2) Page 11. v. G. Fedotov, *Saints of Ancient Russia.*

(3) Page 22. v. Hershenzon's book, *Young Russia.*

(4) Page 30. The Anarchist element is particularly strong in K. Aksakov.

(5) Page 32. v. P. Sakulin, *Russian Literature and Socialism.* 1922.

(6) Page 33. v. P. Sakulin, *op. cit.*

(7) Page 33. See an interesting book by Cornu, *Karl Marx, L'homme et son Œuvre.* 1934.

(8) Page 38. v. *Belinsky's Socialism.* Essays and Letters. Edited and commented by Sakulin, 1925. The remarkable letters from Belinsky to Botkin are collected in this book.

(9) Page 38. See an interesting book recently published, *Hegel bei den Slaven;* about 250 pages are devoted to Hegel in Russia. This part was written by D. Chizhevsky, a great authority on the history of Russian philosophical thought. Insufficient attention is paid to the double crisis of Hegelianism in Russia.

(10) Page 48. See a very interesting book for material about Chernishevsky, *The Love of the People of the 'Sixties.* Academia. 1929.

(11) Page 50. *op. cit.,* p. 61.

(12) Page 52. v. G. Plekhanov, *N. G. Chernishevsky.*

(13) Page 63. v. Michael Bakunin's *Social-politischer Briefwechsel mit Alexander Herzen und Ogarëv,* 1895, in which Nechaev's *Catechism of a Revolutionary* is printed.

(14) Page 65. v. E. Yaroslavsky, *Aus der Geschichte der Kommunistischen Partei der Sowjetunion,* Erst Teil.

(15) Page 66. v. Cornu, *op. cit.*

(16) Page 68. v. M. Bakunin, *The Cat-o'-Nine-Tails German Empire and the Social Revolution.* 1922.

(17) Page 69. *Ibid.*

(18) Page 71. v. G. Plekhanov, *Our Divergencies;* and *A Historical Revolutionary Chrestomathy,* Vol. I. 1923.

(19) Page 74. v. K. Pazhitnov, *The Development of Socialist Ideas in Russia,* Vol. I. 1924.

(20) Page 75. v. A. Voronsky, *Zhelyabov.* 1934.

(21) Page 85. See my book, *Dostoyevsky's Outlook on Life.*

(22) Page 88. See my book, *Konstantine Leontyev, a Sketch of the History of Russian Religious Thought.*

(23) Page 96. v. Cornu, *op. cit.,* and also *Der Historische Materialismus Die Frühschriften,* Kroner. Verlag. In these two recently published volumes Marx's earlier writings are collected.

(24) Page 98. Writing of Feuerbach, Marx says: 'Der Hauptmangel alles bisherigen Materialismus ist dass der Gegenstand, die Wirklichkeit, Sinnlichkeit nur unter der Form des Objects oder der Anschauung gefasst wird, nicht aber als sinnlich-menschliche Tätigkeit, Praxis, nicht subjectiv.' *Thesen über Feuerbach.*

This passage is entirely contradictory to materialism and approaches existential philosophy.

(25) Page 105. Lukatch, *Geschichte und Klassen-Bewusstseit—Studien uber marxistische Dialektik.*

(26) Page 108. My first book, published in 1900, *Subjectivism and Idealism in Social Philosophy,* was an attempt to synthesize revolutionary Marxism and the idealist philosophy of Kant and Fichte.

(27) Page 113. In an article written in 1907 and appearing in my book, *The Spiritual Crisis of the Intelligentsia,* I definitely foretold that if the present great revolution took place in Russia, then it was inevitable that the bolsheviks would triumph.

(28) Page 114. The literature dealing with Russian Communism is immense, but the bulk of it is of no great value. The following may be noted: René Fülöp-Miller, *Geist und*

Gesicht des Bolshevismus; Waldemar Gurian, *Le Bolchevisme*; C. Malaparte, *Le bonhomme Lenine*; Fedor Stepan, *Das Antlitz Russlands und das Gesicht der Revolution*; Berdyaev, *Problème du Communisme*.

(29) Page 116. v. the very able book, *Le bonhomme Lenine,* by C. Malaparte.

(30) Page 116. Lenin's Jubilee Collection.

(31) Page 131. G. de Maistre, *Considérations sur la France.*

(32) Page 149. v. *Historical Materialism,* by various writers of the Institute of Red Professors of Philosophy, under the editorship of Galtsevitch. 1931.

(33) Page 153. N. Fedorov, *The Philosophy of the Common Task.*

(34) Page 155. See the recently published interesting book, *L'idée socialiste,* by Henri de Man.

(35) Page 161. v. *Lenin on Religion.*

(36) Page 166. Yaroslavsky, *On the Anti-Religious Front*; and *Against Religion and the Church.*

(37) Page 167. The matter was dealt with in the journal, *Under the Marxist Flag.*

(38) Page 171. v. Gerard Walter, *Les Origines de Communisme.*

(39) Page 173. Julius Hecker, *Religion and Communism*; and *Moscow Dialogues.*

(40) Page 178. See my *Myself and the World of Objects.*

(41) Page 179. See my *Christianity and the Class Struggle.*

(42) Page 179. I am even inclined to think that in the deep sense of the word the individual is revolutionary and the mass is conservative.

ANN ARBOR PAPERBACKS FOR THE STUDY OF COMMUNISM AND MARXISM

For a complete list of Ann Arbor Paperback titles write:

THE UNIVERSITY OF MICHIGAN PRESS ANN ARBOR